A LETTER FROM PETER MUNK

Since we started the Munk Debates, my wife, Melanie, and I have been deeply gratified at how quickly they have captured the public's imagination. From the time of our first event in May 2008, we have hosted what I believe are some of the most exciting public policy debates in Canada and internationally. Global in focus, the Munk Debates have tackled a range of issues, such as humanitarian intervention, the effectiveness of foreign aid, the threat of global warming, religion's impact on geopolitics, the rise of China, and the decline of Europe. These compelling topics have served as intellectual and ethical grist for some of the world's most important thinkers and doers, from Henry Kissinger to Tony Blair, Christopher Hitchens to Paul Krugman, Peter Mandelson to Fareed Zakaria.

The issues raised at the Munk Debates have not only fostered public awareness, but they have also helped many of us become more involved and, therefore, less intimidated by the concept of globalization. It is so easy to be inward-looking. It is so easy to be xenophobic. It is so easy to be nationalistic. It is hard to go into the unknown. Globalization, for many people, is an abstract concept at best. The purpose of this debate series is to help people feel more familiar with our fast-changing world and more comfortable participating in the universal dialogue about the issues and events that will shape our collective future.

I don't need to tell you that there are many, many burning issues. Global warming, the plight of extreme poverty, genocide, our shaky financial order: these are just a few of the critical issues that matter to people. And it seems to me, and to my foundation board members, that the quality of the public dialogue on these critical issues diminishes in direct proportion to the salience and number of these issues clamouring for our attention. By trying to highlight the most important issues at crucial moments in the global conversation, these debates not only profile the ideas and opinions of some of the world's brightest thinkers, but they also crystallize public passion and knowledge, helping to tackle some of the challenges confronting humankind.

I have learned in life—and I'm sure many of you will share this view—that challenges bring out the best in us. I hope you'll agree that the participants in these debates challenge not only each other but also each of us to think clearly and logically about important problems facing our world.

Peter Munk (1927–2018)
Founder, Aurea Foundation
Toronto, Ontario

THE FUTURE OF CAPITALISM

KATRINA VANDEN HEUVEL AND YANIS VAROUFAKIS VS. ARTHUR BROOKS AND DAVID BROOKS

THE MUNK DEBATES

Edited by Rudyard Griffiths

ANANSI

Published in Canada in 2022 and the USA in 2022 by House of Anansi Press Inc.
www.houseofanansi.com

26 25 24 23 22   1 2 3 4 5

Library and Archives Canada Cataloguing in Publication

Title: The future of capitalism : Vanden Heuvel and Varoufakis vs. Brooks and Brooks / edited by Rudyard Griffiths.
Other titles: Future of capitalism (Toronto, Ont.)

Names: Griffiths, Rudyard, editor. | Vanden Heuvel, Katrina, panelist. | Varoufakis, Yanis, panelist. | Brooks, Arthur C., 1964- panelist. | Brooks, David, 1961- panelist.

Series: Munk debates.
Description: Series statement: The Munk debates
Identifiers: Canadiana (print) 20190228458 | Canadiana (ebook) 20190228482 | ISBN 9781487007430 (softcover) | ISBN 9781487007447 (EPUB) | ISBN 9781487007454 (Kindle)

Subjects: LCSH: Capitalism—Forecasting.

Classification: LCC HB501 .F88 2020 | DDC 330.12/2—dc23

Cover design: Alysia Shewchuk and Ricky Lima
Transcription: Transcript Heroes

House of Anansi Press respectfully acknowledges that the land on which we operate is the Traditional Territory of many Nations, including the Anishinabeg, the Wendat, and the Haudenosaunee. It is also the Treaty Lands of the Mississaugas of the Credit.

Canada Council   Conseil des Arts
for the Arts   du Canada

ONTARIO ARTS COUNCIL
CONSEIL DES ARTS DE L'ONTARIO
an Ontario government agency
un organisme du gouvernement de l'Ontario

With the participation of the Government of Canada | Canadä
Avec la participation du gouvernement du Canada

We acknowledge for their financial support of our publishing program the Canada Council for the Arts, the Ontario Arts Council, and the Government of Canada.

Printed and bound in Canada

CONTENTS

Pre-Debate Interviews with Moderator
Rudyard Griffiths

KATRINA VANDEN HEUVEL IN CONVERSATION
WITH RUDYARD GRIFFITHS

RUDYARD GRIFFITHS: Katrina, great to have you here in Toronto.

KATRINA VANDEN HEUVEL: Thank you, thank you.

RUDYARD GRIFFITHS: You've had a storied career in publishing, in the world of ideas. Of all the many different topics that you could latch onto, why does this issue of capitalism interest you right now?

KATRINA VANDEN HEUVEL: I think it's the recent pivot in the conversation. Particularly since the financial crisis of 2008, which changed so much of our lives, you can look out at the ideas that are now dominating our debate, and they're bold and different, because people saw the structural failure of a system that wasn't working for them. And that was a moment where I think people woke up and said, "We need to do something different; this is not working." Now, it might be capitalism 3.0, it might be social democracy, it might be democratic socialism. But what was on order as of 2008 is now ripped apart.

And what interests me is that even corporate chieftains, even big investors — Ray Dalio of Bridgewater Associates, Marc Benioff of Salesforce, two hundred members of the Business Roundtable — are saying that this kind of capitalism, predatory, extractive, call it what you will, is not working; we need to find different models. Now, some say this because they're worried there'll be pitchforks and protests in the streets — and there are protests — but others are thinking through how to build a more sustainable, more humane, more inclusive capitalism.

RUDYARD GRIFFITHS: It's been ten years since the financial crisis, and some might argue that over that decade, inequality has gotten worse, that features of capitalism that are making working families and working people struggle economically have only gotten more extreme. So, what happened? If you felt that the 2008 crisis marked a kind of wakeup call that the system was in need of reform, why didn't we see that reform after 2008?

KATRINA VANDEN HEUVEL: Reform in America takes time, it zigs and zags. I think 2016 in many ways was the first

4

post–financial crisis election, where you had Bernie Sanders — like him or not — speaking about issues of inequality that needed to be addressed. The big money that rigs the system, that erodes the power of working people, conversations on all of these issues were suddenly jump-started. So, in this upcoming 2020 election, we're seeing a wealth-tax discussion. We're seeing discussions about billionaires, and not just punitive discussions, in my mind, but discussions like: How much power should the very rich have in a society? Does that power mean they write the rules? What do we do about big money? How does it corrupt the very best of American values?

So, it's taken time to get here, but we're having that discussion, and I think that's why this debate is so fraught and vital. We're at a moment where, once again, these issues are on the agenda. In the quick aftermath of 2008, they were kind of swept away, but now we're confronting them again. Inequality has metastasized; there is no question that the very rich are accumulating the wealth in society — that a just tax system needs to be thought through. And there are other measures being discussed and debated, ideas that the *Nation* has championed for decades — a global Green New Deal, Medicare for all, free higher-ed, a fifteen-dollar minimum wage — that you wouldn't have expected to be at the centre of a debate. They were once considered fringe or marginal — not by us — and they're not anymore.

RUDYARD GRIFFITHS: You're no doubt going to hear tonight an argument from your opponents that part of the reason

the capitalist system is successful is because it is so productive, that it spins off all this wealth, and that if you
start to constrain it, if you start to reallocate the distribution of wealth and give that role to the state, that wealth
will no longer exist, and things like Medicare, Medicaid,
and funding for education will be at risk. Do you buy that
argument? Do you think that there is a danger here of
constraining capitalism to the point where it no longer
can fashion the public goods that probably both you and
your opponents would agree on?

KATRINA VANDEN HEUVEL: I certainly agree on the need for
public goods, but I think capitalism as we see it today is
too unconstrained, so unfettered, so deregulated. The idea
that you can't have a vibrant, innovative, free-enterprise
system with an active government is belied by the history of this nation. Some of the most productive periods
in our country's history came in the aftermath of the
Second World War. Sure, there were racial inequalities,
but workers had more power, corporations were thriving,
there was more equality, the ratio between CEOs' pay
and workers' was maybe 26 to 1, and now it's 350 to 1.
So, I think you can have a vibrant free-enterprise system
with regulation that allows for empowerment of working
people and shared prosperity.

There's a cartoon-caricature quality to some of the discussion, where the choice is either free enterprise or state-
controlled socialism. I don't believe that. I think of the
collateral damage caused by predatory, unregulated, unte-
thered capitalism. I know David Brooks believes deeply

in communities, in communitarian instincts, but you can see that communities have been ravaged in many ways by a capitalism that lets factories flee, that doesn't account for the corporate crime of opioid epidemics. There's a lot that can be done within a free-enterprise system within a mixed economy. So, I think it'll be an interesting debate.

RUDYARD GRIFFITHS: Another argument that may come up is the idea that capitalism moves at the speed of light, and, at the press of a button, money can leave the United States or money can choose to come to the United States or Canada. And so if we start to develop systems that put pressures on that capital, it's going to find other jurisdictions that are more friendly to the profit motive. Because what's underneath capitalism is a motive to create profit, to return value to shareholders. What do we do about this in the globalized capitalism that we now live in?

KATRINA VANDEN HEUVEL: Well, first of all, don't listen to just me. You have a lot of corporate executives questioning the primacy of shareholder value; we should think about stakeholder value too. I think one of the reasons we had a financial crisis in 2008 was that money was moving at light speed. I think we could do a lot in this country if we had what I call patient capital, if you had non-speculative, non-nanosecond-moving capital invested in healing our ailing infrastructure and invested in productive returns. That doesn't mean clamping down on capital, but that capital should be moving at slower rates in order to be productive.

And I think, by the way, that a financial transaction tax — which has been on the agenda since James Tobin, the economist in the seventies, raised it — is a brilliant idea, and one the conservative German finance minister has signed on to. A small levy on speculation, which would slow capitalism down a little, but even more would produce revenue for public investments, for public goods. Because I think if it's *all* about profit, it's not a productive society.

RUDYARD GRIFFITHS: Where do you think we're at in this debate right now? Are we near some kind of more significant change in terms of how capitalism exists, its impact, and how it's structured in our societies, or is this going to be a long, slow, grinding set of pitched battles and incremental reforms? Because right now in the United States, you have a presidential election coming up, and you have a political cycle that seems to suggest that there could be the potential for change but also that the status quo is very powerful.

KATRINA VANDEN HEUVEL: Again, reform, especially radical reform, is very tough in any country, and particularly in the United States. But I do think if we had a president come in committed to seeing some of the bold structural ideas we're talking about, they could do a lot by executive action and make some significant changes, even if they didn't have the Senate. But we're already seeing a lot change in an unsexy area, where it doesn't get enough attention: in states and localities.

I think we're on the pivot point, an inflection moment, where we're going to see some changes. It's not going to be status quo, it won't be a grind, but it's going to take struggle; all change takes struggle. Power doesn't concede without demand and struggle, so it's going to take movements allied with leaders inside the system who believe that we need a different kind of capitalism or a social democracy. And, as you well know, and we talked on the phone about this, a younger generation is very interested in — and many are committed to — what they think of as socialism.

Gallup did a poll last year that showed many younger people think of socialism as meaning equality more than state control or ownership of the means of production. So what socialism means to a younger generation is up for grabs. But it's an interesting moment. Coming back to the financial crisis, they may not be old enough to really remember living through it, but they've seen the collateral damage it's caused. They live with student debt that's not sustainable, and they may live at home with parents whose housing mortgages are underwater or not viable.

YANIS VAROUFAKIS IN CONVERSATION WITH RUDYARD GRIFFITHS

RUDYARD GRIFFITHS: Yanis, great to have you here in Toronto.

YANIS VAROUFAKIS: It's very good to be here. Thank you.

RUDYARD GRIFFITHS: I want to start by asking if you could explain what drew you initially to a critique of capitalism? Was it something that your academic work exposed you to? Was it a real-life experience? What made you into this searing critic of the capitalist model?

YANIS VAROUFAKIS: Well, to begin with, I believe that we should always be critical of the world we live in. Whether you live in feudalism, in ancient Athens, or in China, you should always be critical because otherwise there is no scope for improvement. My interest in capitalism dates from before my student days even. I've always been extremely struck with and impressed by capitalists and appalled by them at the very same time. This dialectical, sort of conflictual relationship, has been a driving force in my life.

RUDYARD GRIFFITHS: And you are an academic. You trained and taught as a professor. What did you take out of your academic career, in terms of an appreciation or understanding both of capitalism's power to transform but also, as you feel, its capacity to dehumanize us?

YANIS VAROUFAKIS: What I learned from my experience of teaching in economics departments for decades is that economics has very little to do with capitalism itself. What it has to do with is the fantastic capacity of economists to build gigantic pyramids of modelling without having anything in them that pertains to the essence of capitalism. If you look at the economic models of the world we live in, you'd be struck, if you managed to home in on it, by the fact that some important ingredients are missing. There's no money in economic models of capitalism, there is no debt, and there is no time — because if you introduce time, the mathematics is simply unsolvable.

So how can you have these wonderful minds, all these monoliths of the human intellect, working for so long, getting Nobel Prizes — I'm thinking of Kenneth

Arrow — and yet the models that they build have nothing to do with really existing capitalism. That contrast between reality and a whole profession dedicated to not seeing and yet getting a lot of kudos out of being the experts on capitalism, is just incredible.

RUDYARD GRIFFITHS: Let's go from academia to the real world. You're sitting in the Greek parliament now, and you've had a very active role in Greece's politics since the Eurozone crisis of the last decade, after the 2008 financial crisis. What lessons do you take away from that experience in terms of some of these fundamental faults or defects that you see in the contemporary, so-called late-capitalist era that we're in right now?

YANIS VAROUFAKIS: We live in the great failure of 1971. Do you remember when Richard Nixon proclaimed the end of the Bretton Woods system? That was the end of the twenty-year golden age of capitalism. Bretton Woods was quite remarkable, and it is what created the sense we still have that capitalism is a very successful enterprise. But that broke down in 1971 when Bretton Woods died on us, and ever since we have had multiple crises. In the European Union there's been a frantic effort to replace Bretton Woods with the fixed-exchange-rate regime that led to the euro, which then led to a massive crisis — bubbles that burst and the trials and tribulations of my people, and of the German people, for that matter — today and so on.

It also led to a very interesting global phenomenon,

whereby after 1971, the United States went from being the surplus country, the country that effectively was a creditor nation of the world, to the deficit nation of the world. And those deficits were instrumental in sucking into the United States the net exports of Canada, Japan, Germany, and later China, and creating what we call financialized globalization, which then went into a major spasm in 2008. So, in a sense, we are all children of a permanent crisis that began in 1971.

RUDYARD GRIFFITHS: Let's try some arguments head-on that you're going to hear during this debate. Probably the most prevalent argument for the current capitalist system is its perceived ability to eradicate poverty. And if we look back over the last quarter century or more, we've seen literally hundreds of millions of people lifted out of abject poverty with the introduction of capitalist free-market, free-enterprise-style reforms. Do you accept that that is an enduring positive power and feature of the current capitalist global order?

YANIS VAROUFAKIS: Not just the current system, but capitalism in general. And you don't have to rely on a supporter of capitalism for that argument. Think of Karl Marx. He was the one who eulogized capitalism for having dragged us out of backwardness, out of the superstition of the Middle Ages, out of feudalism —

RUDYARD GRIFFITHS: Out of the "idiocy of rural life" was his quote.

YANIS VAROUFAKIS: Yes, indeed. And having created immense wealth, while at the very same time creating newfangled forms of deprivation and poverty. So the poverty in England of the nineteenth century, the poverty that you have in parts of India now, where the old agrarian society is being transformed by Monsanto and new techniques of production, creating a new social disaster and ecological catastrophe, that's what capitalism is. It is a very interesting force that unleashes fantastic capacities while at the same time creating gigantic crises.

RUDYARD GRIFFITHS: Let's move onto some other arguments that your opponents are no doubt going to bring up tonight. One that they'll point to, when talking about the ecological crisis, is the idea that more prosperous, more capitalistic societies benefit from cleaner environments, and that through innovation, through their ability to create new technologies, capitalism is actually an engine for a cleaner environment — that it is a tool that we need to apply to, not take away from, humanity's confrontation with the crisis of climate.

YANIS VAROUFAKIS: It's a gross mistake to identify capitalism and technology. We need more technologies, not fewer technologies; the more technology the better. The cleaning up of the planet, ecological sustainability, wealth, shared prosperity will all depend on our capacity to have better and more machines. There's no doubt about it. The question is whether what we now call capitalism — *really existing* capitalism, not theoretical capitalism, because there is a profound difference between the two, just as in the Soviet Union there was a fundamental chasm between the theory of communism and the reality of communism—can provide public goods.

What we now have is a gigantic concentration of market power in very, very few corporations and in the very few, shadowy, financial firms that control the corporations. And we have a lot of waste of technological potential. At the same time, the market was never designed to provide public goods; the market was only designed to provide private goods. The environment is a public good. The market will always create profits for the corporations by depleting natural resources, to which the market will always assign a zero price. So the question is: How can you ameliorate for this drive?

Can the state do it? No, because our states, our democracies, have been completely usurped by the concentration of money. And the fact is that our politics has been purchased by those who have an interest in depleting the natural resources of the planet. So, can markets do it? We do need them; we cannot do without them. Can technology? Without technology I wouldn't want to live on this planet, or any other planet for that matter. But the question is: How do we organize economic and social life in a way that allows the markets and those technologies to be freed from corporate abuse?

RUDYARD GRIFFITHS: Let's talk about another aspect of this debate, which will be the supposed political theory that underlies current capitalist thinking, this idea that capitalism and democracy are somehow closely inter-twined and that if you reduce the scope of the free market, if you curtail the opportunities for free enterprise, you're undermining and eroding people's personal freedom.

YANIS VAROUFAKIS: Does anybody believe this?

RUDYARD GRIFFITHS: Well, your opponents tonight are, I think, going to live and die on that.

YANIS VAROUFAKIS: I hope they don't, because then all I will have to do is just utter one word: China. That's it; that's the end of the conversation. China proves that there is no association between capitalism and democracy. And not just China; think of Britain in the late-eighteenth and nineteenth centuries. There was no democracy. Liberalism, remember, was the opponent of democracy. The great liberal thinkers like John Stuart Mill opposed democracy. For them, giving the *demos* the opportunity to decide goes against liberal principles and against the free markets. So, this association of liberalism with democracy is a very recent thing. And it's not doing very well.

The problem is this: capitalism creates not just wealth, as we said before, but also crises that undermine its own sustainability. Since 1929 the democratic politics angle has been essential to stabilizing capitalism. Think of the New Deal in the 1930s; think of every financial crisis that gives rise to a political attempt to pick up the pieces and create social sustainability and economic and financial sus-tainability. So, democracy comes in when capitalism goes through a spasm and falls on its face and cannot get up.

The trouble now is—and you can see this with Donald Trump, you can see it with Brexit, you can see it with authoritarianism gaining all over the place, from Brazil to India, the rise of the Nationalist Internationals, as I call them—that democratic politics is broken and its fate is intertwined with an increasing concentration of corporate power.

RUDYARD GRIFFITHS: Let's talk about increasing concentrations of wealth generally. A big feature of this debate will no doubt be the topic of economic inequality. Thomas Piketty and others have argued that economic inequality is in a sense the status quo of capitalism; it's not an episodic feature but rather something that runs through the capitalist history of the last two hundred years. Is that an idea that you subscribe to?

YANIS VAROUFAKIS: It is definitely the case. The only time when inequality declined was when there was a planned economy in the West—during the Bretton Woods system, for instance, when Franklin Roosevelt effectively banned bankers from being in the Bretton Woods conference and turned banking into plain, regular, boring banking finance.

But my main concern is not so much inequality, which may sound strange coming from a left-winger. My concern comes from the division of society into two classes: those who don't even know what to do with all the money they're accumulating—and you can see how angst-ridden they are with the billionaires calling for the reform of capitalism—and the rest, who are not simply falling behind in relative income or wealth terms but can also see their children living in precariousness and a world in which uncertainty is the order of the day, and in which those children are going to have a far worse life than their parents did. That feeds into discontent. Discontent feeds into anger, and anger feeds into racism, into xenophobia. Peace is in trouble as a result. You can see how easily somebody like Donald Trump can jump on a soapbox and promise people that he's going to make them proud again, that he's going to drain the swamp and so on, and in the end, usurps the power that anger bestows upon him in order to put somebody from Goldman Sachs in charge of the Treasury. That is the reason why the present degree of inequality is symptomatic of a dynamic that makes the society in which we live, especially if you couple it with the ecological damage, unsustainable.

RUDYARD GRIFFITHS: So, this is where I want to end with you. What does the future look like? You know Marx's prediction that capitalism will collapse under its own contradictions, that these extremes will become so extreme that there's a political crisis that follows an economic crisis.

YANIS VAROUFAKIS: This crisis is happening. Europe is ungovernable. I've just arrived from Europe; there is no such thing as Europe anymore—remember what Henry Kissinger said about Europe: "Who do I call?" Look at the United States. Look at global governance; there's no such thing. The World Trade Organization is toast. The

United Nations is a joke. The G7, the G20—they are just gathering places where people exchange insults. So, the political crisis is definitely with us. Racism and xenophobia are on the way up. Everybody talks about the migration crisis when there is no migration crisis. We have the same number of migrants and refugees that we had in 1961; this is a moral panic. What is the future holding for us? I have no idea; nobody knows. This is the wild beauty of indeterminacy. But capitalism is certainly a passing phase, like feudalism was.

There is no such thing as a natural order of things in human society. Technological innovations will make sure of that very soon—with the 3D printer, artificial intelligence, and so on, there will be no reason to have corporations. The economies of scale that sustain General Motors and General Electric will no longer exist. So, what follows? The machines are going to do most of the work, but the question is, are we going to move toward a *Star Trek* society where the machines are working for us and we can explore the universe and have philosophical conversations along the lines of humanism? Or are we going to move toward something closer to *The Matrix*, where we are all serving the machines and are simply victims of a false consciousness that we have created? That's our choice.

ARTHUR BROOKS IN CONVERSATION
WITH RUDYARD GRIFFITHS

RUDYARD GRIFFITHS: Arthur, it's great to have you here in Toronto. I've been looking forward to this.

ARTHUR BROOKS: Thank you, Rudyard. It's wonderful to be here. Always wonderful to be in Toronto.

RUDYARD GRIFFITHS: Let's start with the beginning and how you first became attracted to these ideas of free enterprise, the power of free markets. When did the light turn on for you?

ARTHUR BROOKS: The light turned on for me pretty late. And the reason is that I didn't have a standard background involved with academics and economics, finance, commerce, or business. I come from a family of artists and academics in Seattle, which is practically Canada. We were a progressive family. I don't remember ever having a conversation about capitalism growing up, but I'm sure we were derisive about it. And I didn't go to college, at least not traditionally. I wound up dropping out of college after one year to become a professional classical musician. And that's what I did all the way through my twenties.

But in my late twenties I had a kind of epiphany. I'd wondered what had happened in the world since I was a kid. When I was a child, I had seen grinding poverty, just like all of us did in the early 1970s, in pictures in *National Geographic* magazine. And then when I was touring as a musician as a teenager and in my early twenties, I was going to developing nations and seeing some of the worst poverty I could have imagined. Well, as time went by it seemed like conversations on that level of poverty stopped, that people had lost interest somehow. So as I was getting interested in ideas, I looked into the phenomenon on my own and I found something that shocked me: since 1970, four-fifths of starvation-level poverty had been eradicated.

I, like most Americans and Canadians, was of the view that poverty had gotten worse, because it always seemed to get worse, but it hadn't. I thought, "This is the biggest news; this is incredible. This is a humanitarian achievement on a scale that I couldn't have ever imagined." And I looked into why that was happening. I actually started studying economics by correspondence and wound up getting my bachelor's degree. And, still hungry for the answer, I went back and got my Ph.D. and became an economist, because I thought, two billion of my brothers and sisters had been pulled out of poverty since I was a kid. How do you get the next two billion?

And the answer led me straight on to democratic free enterprise. It was globalization—the much-maligned and hated globalization—that was the solution. It was free trade and the spread of property rights and the role of law and the culture of entrepreneurship. And, in point of fact, those things are what draw people to Canada and the United States, what made *this* into a developed country. As we were seeing their poverty, people around the world were looking at us in Canada and the United States and emulating this system, and they were pulling themselves out of poverty.

It's not perfect. I'm not insane; I don't think capitalism is the only thing that you need. You need rules, you need morals, you need regulation. But my goodness, if I could spread this idea, maybe we can get the next two billion out of poverty.

RUDYARD GRIFFITHS: You've taken spreading this idea a step forward recently with the Netflix documentary *The Pursuit*. What was the impetus behind that?

ARTHUR BROOKS: The impetus behind *The Pursuit* is that I wrote a book called *The Conservative Heart* in 2015, which talked about how we have conservatives, in Canada and the United States, who have certain principles that they always talk about—free enterprise, national security, et cetera. But those values don't mean anything unless they actually start with a proper morality of solidarity in brotherhood, a duty to care for our neighbours. I talked about what dignifies these conservative ideas properly, what's most written on my own heart. Somebody acquired the rights to the book, and a filmmaker wound up following me around the world for three years. And the rest . . . it's not history but at least it's a film on Netflix.

RUDYARD GRIFFITHS: Now, you're going to hear some of your critics tonight. And one obvious argument that they're going to put forward is that, while the capitalist model may have lifted hundreds of millions of people out of poverty, it's creating new and profound inequalities within both developing and developed societies. Maybe more importantly, in our own societies here in the West, we're now seeing this estrangement of the super-rich from the rest, with increasingly profound political impacts. What's your reply to that supposed crisis of our time?

ARTHUR BROOKS: Well, I'm concerned about inequality, just like anybody else. But I have to look at what the facts really say. If you just look at raw income differences, inequality is growing in Canada, in Western Europe, and especially in the United States. But if you look at adjusted income inequality, which is to say, with taxes and transfers and the growth of the welfare state, it's been pretty flat for the past thirty years. Consumption inequality, which measures how much we consume, is dead flat. And worldwide income inequality has been falling for thirty-five years. This is an example of how one measurement shows you something you don't like, but you can't spread it across an entire concept, and you certainly can't spread it around the entire globe.

The thing that concerns me, however, is opportunity inequality, not income inequality. In point of fact, we have a big problem in our societies of people who don't recognize their own dignity. Dignity comes from a sense of worth, a sense of being worthy of respect, and that comes from being needed. And we have too many parts of our societies, especially in the United States, where people have not worked for two and three generations. That concerns me a lot more than income inequality. That's not a product of either socialism or capitalism. It's a problem that all of us, notwithstanding our ideologies and our ideas about politics and economics, need to solve.

RUDYARD GRIFFITHS: Some would say that the state is the right mechanism to solve that, that the solution is to give the state big tools to reach into those communities to create opportunity, maybe through a radical redistribution of wealth.

ARTHUR BROOKS: We do have a lot of redistribution, and I have no beef with people who want more. I may not agree, but I certainly understand those arguments. But the truth of the matter is that the best way to give people a sense of dignity, a sense of being needed, is to allow people to work and pull themselves up. We just don't have very many good state mechanisms to accomplish that. I wish there were better ideas to give everybody a good job, but that's just not what government can do. I have a lot of conservative friends who trash the public sector because the government can't manage these kinds of programs, but that's just not what it's designed to do.

I mean, to give government its due, it's good at redistributing and providing basic services, but it's not good at giving people private-sector employment. That's the reason we need economic growth, so that we can create more jobs, particularly those for people in the margins of society.

RUDYARD GRIFFITHS: Another argument that no doubt will be a feature of this debate is on the impact of capitalism on climate and on the global ecosystem. There's an increasingly vociferous critique of capitalism emerging that says, in a sense, capitalism is poisoning the planet for profit. What's your assessment of that argument?

ARTHUR BROOKS: I don't think that's a strong argument. I understand that there have been all kinds of cases of market failure, where we have pollution, we have environmental spill-over effects, we have climate change, and in many cases those come from cheating the system. These have to do with the fact that government regulation is not strong enough, it's not strenuous enough, we don't have societies that are abiding by proper rules.

But it's also the case that statist economies and societies have much bigger environmental problems than freer societies. And so you find that the worst environmental depredations we've ever seen are in places like the old U.S.S.R. and China. Entire rivers clogged with dead pigs, the worst nuclear disaster in the history of the planet, an entire inland sea drained down to nothing—these happened in socialist economies, while the United States has been getting cleaner, as has Canada, for the past hundred years. Now this doesn't mean that capitalism is perfect, and we do need to do better, to be sure. I'm as concerned as anybody else. But the idea that capitalism is uniquely responsible for poisoning the planet is not an argument that holds water.

RUDYARD GRIFFITHS: Where do you think society is at, in terms of this debate? Because right now in your country, the United States, we're seeing what seems to be a renewed interest in socialism, democratic socialism, or some other form of greater state involvement in life. And we're seeing political candidates like Bernie Sanders and Elizabeth Warren putting forward quite bold proposals that probably would not have had the credibility with voters five years ago that they seem to have today. Is this something new that will be enduring in the American debates?

ARTHUR BROOKS: No, I don't think it is. I mean, I actually don't regret it either. I love a competition of ideas, and the truth of the matter is that you can't make progress when people are not competing in the level of ideas. And I love hearing Bernie Sanders's and Elizabeth Warren's proposals. I can't put forth my own ideas if somebody's not talking about something else. The reason I like the Munk Debates is because we get smart people—well, at least the ones besides me are smart—getting to talk about things that really matter. And in a free society, where nobody's worried and nobody's suffering for their ideas, that's a very beautiful thing. It's what I love about democracy.

I also notice that, in truth, people are talking in a mainstream way about stronger socialist ideas than they have in the past, but the interest in socialism, particularly among young people, is the same as it was twenty-five years ago. I ran the numbers myself and I found that about 58 to 60 percent of people under thirty think socialism is better than capitalism. Well, I thought that too when I was twenty-five years old. So, this is pretty normal, and I'm not deeply worried about it at all.

RUDYARD GRIFFITHS: What do you think the future of free enterprise and capitalism looks like in this era of rapid technological change? Because some people have very dyspeptic views about how atomization, artificial intelligence, and other things could really threaten the capitalist model. The dignity of work, which you've mentioned, is such a core value that could be disrupted. How do you see the future?

ARTHUR BROOKS: The truth is of course that I don't know. If I did, I'd have a hedge fund and be a billionaire, and I'm not. The way that the economy works is quite mysterious to everybody. The surprises per se are kind of what makes it interesting, but I suspect that the kinds of challenges you allude to are going to be the tests of our time.

I don't think that automation is going to make 25 percent of jobs obsolete, which people often say. And the reason for that is because any industrial revolution or any change in the economy, any change in technology, just rearranges people's jobs. Everybody has between twenty and forty tasks in their discrete job; you and I both do. When you take these tasks apart and then put them into new jobs, that looks like a big dislocation in the economy, but it is really just a reorganization. So, I'm not worried that jobs aren't going to exist. What I'm worried about is that people are going to be slow in being able to *do* these new jobs because we're *horrible* at retraining people.

For my money, the problem in the way that we're leaving people behind is not from capitalism or socialism but our lack of imagination in training people, in human capital development. We have education systems in our countries that are appropriate for 1968, and, last I checked, it's 2019 and the needs of the economy are very different than they were in the past.

RUDYARD GRIFFITHS: So why is that? Why isn't the market providing a powerful signal, a powerful cue that's then being responded to? It seems like there is a market failure.

ARTHUR BROOKS: Yes, there's a market failure. But there's actually a government failure. One of the greatest things that the government has ever done is universal public education. It's wonderful, but it's a lumbering tool. It's a beast that moves slowly, and it doesn't react very well to market signals. A private-sector entity would do better under the circumstances, but public-sector education provision, for all its blessings, has not been able to keep up and isn't keeping up today.

DAVID BROOKS IN CONVERSATION
WITH RUDYARD GRIFFITHS

RUDYARD GRIFFITHS: It's my pleasure to welcome here to Toronto *New York Times* columnist and presenter at the Munk Debate on Capitalism, David Brooks.

DAVID BROOKS: It's good to be here.

RUDYARD GRIFFITHS: I want to start with your origin story, so to speak. What drew you to an appreciation for the power that you see in the free enterprise, free-market model? Did you go through an intellectual journey? Because if I look at your biography, your Wikipedia page, it suggests that you didn't start here.

DAVID BROOKS: I was a big socialist in college, and if you go to YouTube and search "Milton Friedman David Brooks," you get a picture of a twenty-one-year-old me as a socialist arguing with Milton Friedman—and getting crushed by him. I was at the time a state socialist. Then I became a police reporter in Chicago, and I covered bad housing policy and bad social policy. There were homes I covered called the Robert Taylor Homes, a housing project, and Cabrini-Green, another big project. And those were built by very well-meaning sociologists and city planners who wanted to improve the lives of the poor. But instead of making things better, they made everything worse.

They tore out all the social fabric and social capital that were in those neighbourhoods, and very quickly they became dangerous poverty traps. I said, it would be great if we could plan the future and just re-engineer society, but that just doesn't work; society's too complicated. So, change has to be incremental and slow, but constant. What I see in capitalism is a learning process. Capitalism sends you price signals, it sends you share prices. If you screw up, it tells you. And so you can constantly learn.

Capitalism isn't my religion; I give it two cheers, not three. It has big downsides, but it involves endless learning, and so it produces better places to live.

RUDYARD GRIFFITHS: Do you subscribe to the idea that capitalism also has this global effect? That over the course of our lifetimes, we have seen the spread of capitalist ideas. Do you see that as a net positive for people around the world? Others, maybe like your debating opponent Yanis

Varoufakis, obviously have a different view of capitalism's effect on the developing world.

DAVID BROOKS: It's a complicated issue, so there's going to be views for both sides. But I see capitalism as having a tremendously positive effect. I covered the Soviet Union — and Russia now is no great place, but the Soviet Union was truly an evil empire that mistreated people in awful ways.

We've seen the greatest reduction in human poverty in human history since 1982, when 48 percent of the world was living in extreme poverty on under two dollars a day. Now that's down to 12 percent. One billion people have been lifted out of poverty. That, to me, is one of the single biggest achievements of our lifetime. And it's not because we got better at planning; it's because China and India and parts of Africa moved in a free-market direction. And the market lifted them up.

And so, the problem with capitalism is that it always causes downsides. It's based on a system of creative destruction, so old things get carved away. And in Canada and in the United States, we see vast differences between the urban and rural. But when you lift a billion people out of severe poverty, you've done something kind of amazing.

RUDYARD GRIFFITHS: Let's talk about some of that creative disruption. You're someone who has written about and taken on board a real concern for the fabric of communities in contemporary society. No doubt an issue that will come up in this debate is the effect of this moment that we're in, "late capitalism," on community. There's a tension in the extent to which these large incumbent corporations operate with disproportionate power on the localities that you philosophically feel give so much enrichment and meaning to our lives. Is that tension resolvable?

DAVID BROOKS: I think it is. The first thing to say is that if you get rid of capitalism, it's not like you return to nirvana. You end up centralizing power in your political elites. One of the nice things about capitalism is that it decentralizes power. You have a power node in politics, a power node in the business sector, and a power node in civic society. And in my view, capitalism can really destroy communities, because capitalism is all about movement and change and opportunity, and people want to move to better things.

When I go around this country and in the U.S., and I look at the health of the fabric of the communities, one of the first things I ask is, "Do the people who own the big employers live *here*?" And when you find a place where a lot of the big employers live in the town and use their wealth to help the community, you see tremendous benefits. And so capitalism, if it's distant and ruthless, can strain communities. But if it's local and active and if you get small groups of businesspeople creating a community foundation, you can have a tremendously positive effect. It's up to the people to behave well.

RUDYARD GRIFFITHS: Do you think people have a right to

stay in their communities, or do they in a sense have to follow these price cues to look for employment and opportunity? Some might ask, do we have a moral responsibility to allow them to exist where they exist, living in ways they might have done for decades or centuries.

DAVID BROOKS: Right. I go around West Virginia, let's say, or you could go out west here in Canada, and there are no jobs in a lot of those places. And you want to say, "Well, you can move." And sometimes they say, "Well, if you can give me a voucher, I'd move. I just can't afford to." I support mobility vouchers for that reason. Sometimes they say, "No, my people are here, my roots are here. I've been here for centuries." And then the right thing to say is, "What can we do to improve this place?"

There's an economist in America named Raj Chetty who studies social mobility and economic health, neighbourhood by neighbourhood. And the amazing thing is that these indicators vary tremendously across neighbourhoods. The neighbourhood is the unit of change. If you have a good school system, strong social institutions, and intact families, you're going to have a neighbourhood where people can do well.

RUDYARD GRIFFITHS: Is there a place for redistributing wealth so that the government has greater resources to provide those types of services?

DAVID BROOKS: Yes. I think one of the mistakes journalists made—and you know, I worked in the *Wall Street Journal* editorial page—was that we thought that every time you increase the size of the state, you decrease the dynamism of the marketplace. But it's very important to distinguish between supportive state action, like education or the great thing Canada has done with child credits, versus regulatory state action, when the government elites actually get in the middle of corporations to determine the decisions they're going to make.

RUDYARD GRIFFITHS: Are you thinking, for example, of corporations controlled by workers sitting on boards, a type of reform that we've seen in Europe?

DAVID BROOKS: I think you can have that to some extent, but if you have political elites essentially making decisions, if you don't have a stock market, you can't tell who's doing well and who's not, then you really damage the workings of the market.

So I looked at Scandinavia, and they have big, generous, supportive welfare states, and they can have those, because they have truly free economies. They have no corporate taxes, minimum wages, or inheritance tax, and they have school choice. It was a mistake to think the central argument was big government versus big market. You can have big market and big government, so long as it's the right kind of supportive government.

RUDYARD GRIFFITHS: What's your prescription for economic inequality? Because economists like Thomas Piketty have argued that it is a structural feature of capitalism; it's not the exception, it's the rule. And if you look at the latest numbers from the United States, inequality seems to be getting worse, not better. Based on your model of maintaining these market cues and having the efficiency of market mechanisms, how do you address such a big, challenging problem like economic inequality without, again, risking giving power to these political elites to sort it out for all of us?

DAVID BROOKS: It's worth pointing out that over the last thirty years we've seen the greatest reduction in global wealth inequality in history. What we have is people in Malaysia and Vietnam getting much closer to people in Canada and the United States. The disadvantage of that great achievement is that low-skilled or working-class workers in places like Canada and the United States are suddenly competing against people in India. And so you have a distribution of income that they call the "elephant curve," which shows that most income earners are doing really well, but then the graph goes down like the tusk and the trunk of an elephant—and that's the working class not doing well—and then it goes up again for the wealthiest.

So we just need to have programs to help those at the bottom. And one of the things that I think should be done is a change in our education system, which just has not kept up with our technology. We have to have early childhood education, human capital policies all the way through life.

One of the things you notice about inequality is that

it is rising. That is also a product of productivity. There are a number of people, especially in urban places like this, rather than in D.C. or in New York, who are just super-producers. They marry people who are also well educated. They pour tons of resources into their kids. Those kids grow up, and some of them work in banks around here at eighty-to-a-hundred-hour-a-week jobs. And those people are making a lot of money, but they're like slaves to their jobs.

I wouldn't necessarily recommend it, but that's one of the drivers of at least the top chunk of inequality. And I don't want to punish them; I just want to make it so that everybody can have the opportunity to work in a place like that, if they want to. Or get into a trade so they can be productive. You can't fix inequality without giving more people more skills to become more productive.

RUDYARD GRIFFITHS: Put your U.S. political observer hat on: How would you characterize this moment that we're in, where we're seeing some real energy around these ideas of democratic socialism and greater wealth redistribution? Is it something real and enduring now in American politics, or is this a flash that maybe is simply a reaction to Trump or to the financial crisis?

DAVID BROOKS: Well, a lot of things are happening. My general answer is that Trump was the wrong answer to the right question. A lot of people in rural places have seen their communities torn apart by a culture of hyper-individualism. And so, they've seen the places they love fall and they say, I've got to make some changes. And then a lot of young people have now, in the U.S., a huge amount of student debt. There are real problems, as there always are in capitalism. The question I would ask is: Are we going to swap it out for something new?

I would ask people to walk around Toronto and ask, Is this such a crisis that we need to swap it all out? I'd ask them to look at the national income statistics and see that Canadian wages are growing by 4.5 percent a year. Is that such a crisis that we want to swap it out? My wife has worked in Hamilton, Ontario. Hamilton has been hit by a bad economy, but it can recover, and capitalism is great at innovation. I do think there are fundamental challenges, but I personally don't think it's such a crisis that we want to rip it out and hand it over to a system that has failed every time it's been tried. I mean, the weird thing about this debate is, we have 150 years of history here. It's not theoretical; we've run the program and capitalism won.

If you look at the actual world, the central debate in our time is between democratic capitalism in places like this and authoritarian capitalism in places like China. It's capitalism either way; are we going to make it good capitalism or bad capitalism?

The Future of Capitalism

Be it resolved: The capitalist system is broken. It's
time to try something different . . .

Pro: Katrina vanden Heuvel and Yanis Varoufakis
Con: Arthur Brooks and David Brooks

December 4, 2019
Toronto, Ontario

RUDYARD GRIFFITHS: Ladies and gentlemen. Welcome to the Munk Debate on Capitalism. My name is Rudyard Griffiths. It's my privilege to have the opportunity to help organize this debate series and to once again serve as your moderator.

I want to start by welcoming the North America–wide television audience tuning in to this debate right now on CPAC, Canada's public affairs channel. And with our partners in the United States, WNED and their PBS sister stations. It's great to have you as part of the program. A warm hello also to our online audience watching right now at munkdebates.com and via the website of our exclusive social media partner, Facebook. Thank you for tuning in.

And finally, hello to you, the over 3,000 people who've filled Roy Thomson Hall for yet another Munk Debate. On behalf of the Munk Foundation and all of us working at the debates, we so appreciate your support for more and better debates of the big issues of the day.

Now, tonight is a bit of a milestone for this series. This evening marks our twenty-fifth consecutive debate. Quite an accomplishment—twenty-five debates. That's pretty good. Our ability, year in and year out, to bring to this stage some of the world's sharpest minds and brightest thinkers would not be possible without the public spiritedness and the generosity of our founders and hosts tonight, the Aurea Foundation and the Munk family. Thank you for keeping this series going. I think Peter would have enjoyed this debate. I'm sure he would have had a few opinions about it.

So, why are we convening this debate now? Of all the various topics we could have confronted this autumn, why did we turn to capitalism? Well, something is clearly happening in our politics and in our culture when it comes to public perceptions of free markets, capitalism, and free enterprise. More and more of our fellow citizens have come to believe, quite simply, that the capitalist system no longer works. They blame it for fuelling rising, if not rampant, economic inequality and stagnating living standards. They believe, many strongly, that capitalism is poisoning the planet for profit. And they are genuinely worried about how capitalism is concentrating in the hands of a few wealthy and powerful elites increasing amounts of democratically unaccountable power. In short, I don't think it's a stretch to say we're living through a moment when we as a society are experiencing a crisis of faith in capitalism as an engine of economic, social, and human progress.

But, as we'll hear tonight, capitalism's defenders feel that blaming the capitalist system for society's problems is the moral panic of our time. They see free markets rightly as having lifted hundreds of millions of people out of abject poverty around the world. They believe that capitalism is a powerful tool to clean up the environment, to spread human rights, to promote political liberty, and to encourage all the kinds of technological breakthroughs that have made our lives immeasurably better. We know that.

For capitalism's proponents, the answers to these real and urgent problems that our society faces, such as the environment and economic inequality, is more liberty, more free markets—in short, more capitalism.

So tonight we challenge the essence of these arguments by posing a simple motion, "Be it resolved: the capitalist system is broken; it is time to try something different."

Arguing in favour of tonight's motion is one of the world's leading socialist democratic thinkers. He's a member of the Greek parliament—I think he's got a budget coming out tomorrow that he's going to have to comment on—he was finance minister of Greece during the Eurozone crisis, and he's an internationally bestselling author. Ladies and gentlemen, please welcome to Toronto, Canada, Yanis Varoufakis. Thank you, Yanis. Thank you.

Well, one great debater deserves another, and Yanis's debate partner tonight is one of America's leading progressive voices. She is the publisher of the storied *Nation* magazine, a *Washington Post* columnist, and the acclaimed author of numerous books on economics, politics, and international affairs. Ladies and gentlemen, Katrina van-den Heuvel.

Speaking against the motion is Harvard professor, best-selling author, and the star of the Netflix hit documentary *The Pursuit*—ladies and gentlemen, Arthur Brooks.

Joining Arthur on the Con team for this debate is the celebrated *New York Times* columnist, author, and the person we turn to regularly on PBS stations to try to understand the big issues of our time. Ladies and gentlemen, please welcome our final presenter, David Brooks.

It's now time for us to have our first audience vote on the resolution, "Be it resolved: the capitalist system is broken; it's time to try something different." And here are some preliminary numbers. Interestingly, public opinion in this hall, I would say, is virtually split within the margin of error: 47 percent in favour of the motion, 53 percent opposed. So, we certainly have a debate on our hands.

Now we're going to see how fluid opinion is in this audience. We're going to ask you a second question: Are you open to changing your vote over the next hour and a half? Is there something that either one of these teams of debaters could say that could conceivably let you vote in a different way when we come to our final vote on the resolution at the end of tonight's debate? Let's see those results: 79 percent are open to changing their minds. So, we have an audience of creative thinkers who are willing to consider what they hear from these two teams with sharply diverging points of view.

Let's move now to opening statements. We're going to

have six minutes on the clock for each one of the debaters. And, according to debating convention, we're going to have the team arguing for the resolution speak first. Yanis Varoufakis, you have six minutes on the clock. Let's have your opening words.

YANIS VAROUFAKIS: Good evening, Toronto. Good evening, ladies and gentlemen. We have a great debt of gratitude to capitalism. Capitalism liberated us from prejudice, superstition, backwardness, feudalism. But at the same time, we owe capitalism blame for unbearable inequality, unsustainable debt, brazen authoritarianism, and, yes, catastrophic climate change.

There's no doubt that capitalism produced immense wealth, but it produced it on the same — exactly the same — production line on which it manufactured new forms of deprivation. It lifted billions of people from poverty, but it created new forms of desperation for many others.

When asked who is the worst enemy of capitalism, I never respond by pointing to the Left. We leftists are a bunch of losers. We have a tendency to fall prey to authoritarianism — look at the Soviet Union. Capitalism is not threatened by the Left.

The liberals look to all these billionaires who are now angst-ridden, watching their stash of cash rise exponentially while wondering how they will enjoy it in a world in which the majority are sliding into precarity. They are not going to change anything either because, however much money they give away, they will never do anything to jeopardize the dynamic process by which their privileges are being reproduced.

What about liberals? American liberals? Small-*l* liberals, or social democrats in Europe? They're also impotent because they have their own diagnosis. They think that the problem with capitalism is that, on our behalf, it has purchased efficiency at the expense of injustice. No. The problem with capitalism is that it is particularly inefficient at using the fantastic technologies and wealth that it produces. The problem with capitalism at the moment is that it is seriously undermining itself, and so becomes its own worst enemy. It is undermining humanity's capacity to share the prosperity of planet Earth.

Remember the Soviet Union? That awful contraption? It has as much to do with the principles of socialism as today's really existing capitalism has to do with free-market ideology — nothing whatsoever. We do not live in a small-town, front-porch community where the butcher, the brewer, and the baker, through acting in their self-interest, pursue the common good. We live in a very, very different kind of world.

We live in a really existing capitalism, which is against free markets. It has been against free markets since the invention of electromagnetism, which gave rise to the Edisons, the Fords, the grids, the network companies, the mega-companies, the big business cartels that were fantastic at usurping states, replacing markets, and fixing prices against the interest of their own supposed ideology. It is anti-liberal. It is compelling young people today to think of themselves as brands instead of as human beings — if they are not obliged to work zero-hour contracts under wages that make the idea of personal freedom, personal space, and personal development a cruel joke.

Really existing capitalism today is utterly inefficient. Think of the mega-banks that were necessary to fund the mega-corporations, how they have created fictitious capital based on mountain ranges of debt—of unsupportable debt that periodically goes through a spasm. Think of what has been happening since the financial collapse of 2008, where we have a world today with the highest level of savings in the history of humanity, and the lowest level of investment in the things that are essential for human dignity and for the planet.

And really existing capitalism is profoundly anti-democratic. We have captains of industry and masters of finance who accumulate war chests with which they effectively buy politics, buy campaigns, and capture regulators.

Ecological destruction is an essential aspect of this techno-structure. Markets were never designed to protect public goods like the environment. They were only designed to create private goods. There is no way that this corporatized, financialized capitalism that we live in can ever value the scarce resources of our nature, of our environment. This capitalism will assign a near-zero price to it and therefore deplete it until it's gone.

Ladies and gentlemen, the really existing capitalism that we live in has a lot more to do with the Chinese Communist Party than Adam Smith. It is based on this grand divide between those who work in corporations but have no power, and those who have power but do not work in the corporations. Think about Google. An employee of Google, the moment they enter Google, however happy they may be on campus, they exit the market. They enter an economic planned system. It's a bit like the Gosplan, the Soviet planning system, only with brighter colours and better food. And think about our great corporations like Apple, General Motors, Ford. They're more like hedge funds that manufacture some stuff.

RUDYARD GRIFFITHS: Arthur Brooks, you're up first for the Con team. Six minutes on the clock for you.

ARTHUR BROOKS: Thank you. What an honour it is to be here with my partner, David Brooks. We have lots of Brookses on our side. And Yanis and Katrina, on the other side, are people I have tremendous respect for and have had for many years.

I'm on the capitalism side of this debate because poverty is the thing I care about the most. I was raised in a politically progressive family in Seattle, Washington, which is practically Canada. I made my living as a musician all the way through my twenties. I neither knew nor cared about economics and held no brief whatsoever for the free-enterprise system. But I had a question that always nagged at me. I remember the haunting images of poverty that came from the East African famine of the early 1970s when I was a young boy. It was the first time most Canadians and Americans had ever seen the face of true, grinding poverty—the boy with flies on his face and a distended belly in *National Geographic* magazine. You remember it; so do I. It haunted me, and you. I wanted to know what could be done, but the implication was that nothing could be done, that the world couldn't get better.

Well, I grew up, and it seemed like the attention paid to that boy and the poorest people in the world had waned. I asked, had he been forgotten? Had the poorest been forgotten?

In my early thirties, I decided to find the answer to what had happened to the poorest people in the world since I was a child. And I found something that shocked me and changed my life.

I had assumed, like two-thirds of Americans and probably most Canadians do, that poverty had gotten worse since I was a child. I was wrong. According to the best data in the world, compiled by the World Bank and economists at MIT and Columbia University, since 1970 when I was a young child, four-fifths of starvation-level world poverty has been eradicated.

Even living on a dollar a day or less, adjusted for inflation, there has been an 80 percent decline in poverty, for the first time in human history. That is a humanitarian achievement beyond our wildest dreams.

I had to know *why*. I was a musician, but I became an economist—from the sublime to the dismal—to find out why. By the way, as a musician I never would have had the opportunity to play this hall!

Two billion of my brothers and sisters had been pulled out of poverty since I was a young child. What happened? I'm going to tell you, because I found the secret. And if we know the secret, we can do it again, because we need the next two billion and the next two billion. My friends, it's in our hands.

Five forces did this: globalization, much maligned today; free trade, despised on the Right and the Left; property rights; the rule of law; and the culture of entrepreneurship that brought your ancestors to this great country — that pulled two billion of your brothers and sisters out of poverty. That, my friends, is the essence of how capitalism saves lives.

Now, I am no radical. I will not stand up here and tell you that we need no regulations. I will not tell you that we do not need reform. I will not tell you that capitalism is perfect, because it isn't. But let's remember the truth here.

This is not a partisan or political statement. We have a humanitarian opportunity to repeat the achievements of the past fifty years. Not by getting rid of capitalism, or even curbing capitalism. No, we need to spread capitalism more widely. We need to push it into the corners of the world where it doesn't exist. Why? Because people need to throw off the tyranny of their poverty and the tyranny of the leaders who want to hold them down in statist regimes so that they cannot live up to their God-given potential. Like your ancestors did, the people who came to Canada to give you a better life. Capitalism built that. Not alone. But capitalism was there at its essence.

Now, when I say this is not a political statement, I need you to believe me. Let me read you a quote from somebody I admire a great deal: "The free market is the greatest producer of wealth in history. It has lifted billions of people out of poverty." That's not a quote from

Ronald Reagan. That's not a quote from Boris Johnson. My friends, that's a quote from President Barack Obama in a conversation that we had together on the debate stage at Georgetown University in 2015.

Let me leave you with this. Tonight we're debating whether we should turn our backs on capitalism. As I said before, reform it, find better ways to regulate it, tax people more. I won't like it, but this is democracy. It's fine.

But to turn our backs on capitalism per se is to turn our backs on the people around the world whom we've never met and will never see, but whom we have the privilege of lifting up with our system, with the gift to the world that is our values of freedom and competition. To reject that is to pull the ladder up behind us. It's not right.

It is our privilege to live in a time and an economic system that, despite its flaws, has lifted up so many. If we let it, if we share it, if we spread it widely, then we can—we will—lift up the next two billion people together. Thank you.

RUDYARD GRIFFITHS: Thank you, Arthur. So, Katrina, we're going similarly to put six minutes on the clock for you, and the hall is yours.

KATRINA VANDEN HEUVEL: Good evening. Capitalism is often equated with freedom, free markets, and democracy, but my country's extractive capitalism is deepening inequality, undermining freedom, endangering democracy, and ravaging nature. We urgently need an alternative to the current broken capitalist system that will enable all people, not just the ultra-rich, to live lives of dignity and well-being.

53

Don't you often find that the debate over the economic system is stuck in cartoon caricatures? It's as if we're only offered two choices: robber-baron capitalism, or freedom-zapping state socialism. In this debate I hope we can get beyond these cartoon characterizations. We've lived in mixed economies since the Second World War, with mistakes, but also receiving many clues as to how to best organize our lives. As a result, there are many flavours of capitalism, some more palatable than others. But for forty years we have experienced the global spread of what I would call a neo-liberal flavour and a well-funded attack on government's role as a moderating, countervailing force.

There is also a Canadian-style capitalism, with stronger protections and rules to protect the common good and public investments to reduce poverty and encourage social mobility and innovation. And there's the flavour of Nordic capitalism, of Western European capitalism with a robust social safety net, what I call a decency floor.

Now, hailing from the United States, I care about transforming, rewiring, reimagining our extractive capitalism to create different outcomes, because, as I see it, there are three major ways U.S. capitalism is broken: it is fuelling extreme inequality; it is consuming democracy; and it is destroying nature.

And we've lived through four decades of stagnant wages. We still have stagnant wages and staggering levels of upward flows of wealth that have super-charged the existing racial wealth divide and other inequalities rooted in gender and geographic differences.

So, my appeal to you Canadians—as I witness what is

happening with declining social mobility, what even the Brooks Brothers rightly acknowledge as a serious problem in the United States — is to protect what you have.

The American Dream has moved to Canada, where there is now twice the level of social mobility than in the United States. The good news is that we're having a long-overdue debate about what will best protect our democracy and economy from plutocratic takeover and challenge the concentrated power undermining our democratic norms and institutions.

Now, just about now you may hear a billionaire wailing — perhaps even the first trillionaire freaking out about a wealth tax that would seek that the ultra-rich pay their fair share. I believe my country would be far better off if we had fewer billionaires and many more thousand-aires. Most families don't have $500 in the bank. They can't even pay their health care deductibles. I don't begrudge people who have done well and are all set. But please know that most Americans are a long way from being set.

But you don't have to take it from me. Listen to some of our leading business leaders and investors who have seen the cracks emerging in contemporary capitalism. You may have heard the CEO of Salesforce, who said that capitalism as we know it is dead. Two hundred executives of the Business Roundtable stated this past August that business leaders need to look beyond shareholder return to stakeholder return to ensure that benefits flow to employees, workers, communities, and the planet.

To be clear, the next system I'm talking about isn't a tweak of capitalism, adding a few more regulations and safety nets and green technologies. It is a deep, systemic, structural redesign of basic institutions and functions — from ownership, banking, finance, resources — so that the economy serves the common good and protects the Earth. We may not call the next system capitalism, or even capitalism 3.0, but we probably won't call it socialism either. So, what are the next system's characteristics?

There will be individual freedoms, private enterprises, vibrant small businesses protected from monopoly power. It will include different ownership systems, both broader individual wealth ownership and worker ownership of businesses. And there will be flourishing new business models. Do you know about B Corporations? I think they're terrific. They're benefit companies that recognize multiple stakeholders. There are almost three hundred such corporations in Canada.

What are some steps that would move us in the right direction? We need what I call a plutocracy prevention program — not to be punitive but to protect democracy and ensure that billionaires pay more in taxes than public school teachers and nurses. Such fair, just taxes will raise substantial revenue for vital public investments that will foster opportunity. This was the formula for U.S. social mobility after the Second World War. The next system would include the strengthening of a public banking and investment system designed for what I call patient investment, not speculative capital, to rebuild our decaying infrastructure. It will require planning alongside markets. It will mean rewriting the rules of a rigged system. It will demand limits on wasteful consumption, especially among the world's richest 10 percent. This is not the road to serfdom.

RUDYARD GRIFFITHS: Thank you, Katrina. Okay, let's move to our final opening statement. David Brooks, you have six minutes on the clock.

DAVID BROOKS: Thank you. So, there are four debaters on this stage, only one of which was born in Toronto, Canada. That should not be the only reason you vote for our team, but it should be a major reason.

I was a socialist in college. I read magazines like the *Nation*. If you go to YouTube and search "David Brooks Milton Friedman," you'll see a twenty-one-year-old socialist David Brooks debating Milton Friedman on TV. I had these big 1980s glasses that look like they're on loan from the Palomar Mountain observatory. And even today I get the appeal of socialism and alternatives to capitalism. Why do we have to live with such inequality and poverty? Why can't we put people over profits? Socialism is the most compelling secular religion of all time.

My socialist sympathies did not survive long when I became a journalist. I quickly noticed that the government officials I was covering were not capable of planning the society they hoped to create. That wasn't because they were stupid or bad. Society is just too complicated.

I came to realize that capitalism is really good at doing something socialism is really bad at—creating a learning process to help people figure stuff out. If you want to run a rental car company, capitalism has a whole bevy of market and price signals that tell you what kind of cars people want to rent, how many cars to order, where to put locations. It has a competitive profit-driven process to motivate you to learn and innovate every day.

Socialist planned economies interfere with price and other market signals in a million ways. They suppress the profit motives that drive people to learn and improve. It doesn't matter how big your computer is; you can never gather all the relevant data from a central place. The state cannot even see the tiny, irregular, local context–driven variables that make all the difference. The state cannot predict people's desires. Capitalism creates a relentless learning system; socialism doesn't.

The sorts of knowledge that capitalism produces are often not profound, but they produce enormous wealth. All of human history had basically a flat living standard until capitalism; now it's seen a 10,000 percent rise.

According to the Fraser Institute, a free-market think tank that ranks nations according to the things that free-market think tanks like—less regulation, free trade, secure property—the freest capitalist economies in the world are Hong Kong, Singapore, New Zealand, Switzerland, the United States, Canada, Ireland, the United Kingdom, Australia, and Mauritius. And these free countries' average per capita income is $36,770; in the least free, it's $6,000. In the most-free economies, people live to be 79.4 years old; in the least free it's 65 years.

Over the past century, planned economies have produced enormous amounts of poverty and scarcity. What's worse is what happens when political elites realize what they can do with a scarcity; they can sell it. If things are scarce in such a system, you have to bribe people to get it. Soon everybody's bribing, and citizens soon realize the whole system is a fraud. Socialism produces more economic and political inequality than capitalism because the rulers turn into gangsters. A system that begins in high idealism ends in corruption, dishonesty, and oppression.

I've never been a libertarian free marketer. I'm a Whig. My hero is Alexander Hamilton — who's a Puerto Rican hip-hop star from New York! He came into a country where land-rich oligarchs like Thomas Jefferson had all sorts of means to control wealth. So he said we needed to create broader and fairer capitalism. He created credit markets to do that.

My next hero is Abraham Lincoln, who gave more speeches about banks than about slavery. He said, I want poor boys and girls like me to rise and succeed. We need to create railroads; we need to create the land-grant colleges with which we can educate people to become capitalists.

The final Whig in American politics is Teddy Roosevelt, who loved the energy that capitalism developed and knew you sometimes had to limit capitalism so that everybody could be a fair capitalist.

Some parts of our economic system are in good shape. Wages in this country are rising by 4.5 percent a year. But capitalism, like all human systems, has problems. We could do a lot of things to fix them. We need worker reforms. We need worker co-ops to build skills and represent labour at the negotiating table. We need wage subsidies so people are not swept away by the creative destruction of the free market. We need a carbon tax to use capitalist mechanisms to fight global warming. And all these ideas I've just cited come from places like the American Enterprise Institute and the Brookings Institution that are supposedly the detritus of economic neo-liberalism.

The big mistake those of us on the conservative side made was to equate all government action as part of one thing. But government action comes in two varieties. There's supporting government action, which helps people become better capitalists, and then there's regulation, which gets in the gears of capitalism and screws things up. In Scandinavia they do a lot of supporting capitalism. And they have completely free economies — extremely free economies. They can only afford the supporting capitalism because they have free capitalist economies.

The answer to the current problems is found in fixing our economy, making a wider capitalist economy, a fairer capitalist economy, not in "something else." Thank you.

RUDYARD GRIFFITHS: Thank you. So, we have some sharply divergent views here. We're now going to give our teams the opportunity to rebut what they've heard from the opening statements before we move into our moderated middle of the debate.

Yanis Varoufakis, you started first, so let's put a couple of minutes on the clock for you, and you can provide the audience with your rebuttal of Arthur and David.

YANIS VAROUFAKIS: Capitalism doesn't just have problems. Capitalism is broken. There is no doubt that we would not have civilization if we didn't have capitalism. But that's not the issue. The issue is whether capitalism can continue to evolve as it is of its own accord. It cannot, for two reasons.

First, the crisis of 2008 has already proven to us that the financial system is broken and that the manner in which states have tried to pump up the liquidity from central banks is making a bad thing worse. It's like giving cortisone to a cancer patient. It doesn't help except by simply perking up the patient.

Second, we have a remarkable disconnect between the capacity of our technologies to produce wealth and the capacity of societies to absorb the products of the machines. Very soon, with robotization, society is not going to be able to purchase the goods that it produces. This is why capitalism is well and truly broken.

Let's agree that capitalism has been a force for good. Let's agree we need more markets. Let's agree that we need more freedom. Let's agree that we need more democracy and more liberty. But the only way to do this is by beginning to imagine a transition that we will effect through planning to a different way of running our corporations. Imagine just for a moment a corporation in which every worker, every employee, has one share and one vote. Imagine a situation where we all have an account with our central bank. Imagine a society where every baby that is born gets a trust fund. Imagine a system where we have more democracy by having fewer elections and more lotteries by which to select our authorities.

ARTHUR BROOKS: I agree with so much of what our inter-locutors have said today. And I don't even have to pander to you by being from Toronto!

Yanis's main objection to capitalism is that it turns out to be fundamentally undemocratic. And he's given many examples. The trouble is that that's not capitalism. That's a failure of capitalism. All of the predations that people give of capitalism are the equivalent of the Boston Red Sox blowing up the Yankees' bus on the way to the game. That's not competition; that's shutting competition down.

So, I agree we need true competition. But that doesn't mean that planning is the solution. On the contrary. I think his argument at the end is the strongest. We need more markets pushed to more people at the margins of society. We need more ownership. We need more people in capital markets, including the poor. That's where our minds should go. How can we get not *less* capitalism, but how can we get *more*?

Now, Katrina's excellent argument points out the trouble we have with billionaires, that the inequality is so bothersome, it's so troublesome. And it's not just aes-thetic; it seems that our society has become increasingly unfair. But I *will* point out one incredibly important fact, at least to me, which is that inequality worldwide has been in decline for thirty-five years straight.

Why? Because people at the margins in the poorest countries have pulled themselves up. That doesn't mean that we don't have a problem with inequality in our own societies today. But what is the reason for that? Once again, it's not billionaires per se; it's the unfair ways that some people have acquired and maintained their fortunes. Inevitably, they have not played by the rules, have not been exposed to competition, and in point of fact have not played by capitalism's core tenets in the first place.

KATRINA VANDEN HEUVEL: Thank you, Arthur, for commending my argument.

You mentioned the rules, people who play by the rules, who work by the rules. But the rules have been bought by the very richest, and we need to de-rig the rules so that there's a fair, level playing field. There's a mountain of interdisciplinary research about how extreme inequalities of income, wealth, and opportunity undermine everything that we care about. And that is at the root of a capitalism that is no longer working.

There are different alternative models, as I said. Call it what you will—inclusive capitalism, capitalism with a conscience, regenerative economy, capitalism 3.0—but if you care about democracy, if you care about public and personal health, social cohesion, economic stability, mental health, even sports and culture, the vast inequalities of income, of power, are damaging our society and economy.

I know that David Brooks is a communitarian. And I believe there is a principle—a Christian principle—of subsidiarity, and there's a solidarity principle. As you may know, around the world, and particularly in America at this moment, communities are being ravaged by de-industrialization, by factories leaving, by opioid epidemics, which the public health system is incapable of caring for. That is a by-product, a collateral damage of a capitalist system that values profits over people. And I think we need to pay attention to that.

And to close with Arthur Brooks's compelling statement about global poverty, it's a great quote, it's a quote Arthur used in the famous 2015 conversation with Barack Obama.

But a group many of you know, Oxfam International, have a somewhat more nuanced response to the issue of global poverty, of lifting billions out of poverty. Yes, there has been a decline in extreme poverty thanks to global efforts. But much more could have been done.

DAVID BROOKS: There are two parts to this debate that our opponents need to argue to pull the day. The first is that capitalism is so rotten we need to burn it down. And the second is that they have to offer something else, some alternative.

Walk around Toronto. Do you think we should burn this down? All that's been achieved here? Walk around Canada. I know there are poor parts in the rural areas, we have that too. We have strengths and we have weaknesses. But we're some of the most successful societies on Earth. Burning that down strikes me as a mistake.

The greatest solutions to inequality, to despair, are education, human capital, social support, and decent lives.

America is growing — the poorest earners' wages in America are rising twice as fast as everybody else's because we're finally increasing high school graduation rates. In this country we've reduced poverty by 20 percent recently, partly because of the child tax credit. And there are ways to fix the problems that still exist by pouring resources into early childhood education, nurse-family partnerships, better job training, better community colleges. That is the way you grow.

Now the second thing: Is there an alternative? Do we look in the stew and see B Corps as an alternative? I love B Corps. There are almost three hundred in Canada. And they're capitalist.

The fact is, we haven't said anything new here. We've been having this debate about planning versus the market for 150 years. We've run this experiment. The market won, for all its flaws.

The key debate right now in the world is not between capitalism and socialism; it's between fair democratic capitalism like you have here in Canada, and authoritarian capitalism as in China. The argument is, how do we make our capitalism more democratic? Because there really is no alternative. Thank you.

RUDYARD GRIFFITHS: We're going to do another round of rebuttals because my sense here is that you're starting to probe some of each other's key arguments. So, let's put another two minutes on the clock. Yanis, you're up first.

YANIS VAROUFAKIS: Nobody wants to tear anything down. When we moved from feudalism to capitalism, we didn't tear down the great cathedrals; we just moved on to a new phase of our evolution, a more advanced phase, which was capitalism.

Where we are at now is a serious juncture. We are

destroying the planet at rates that the generation that are teens today are going to hold us responsible for. The market is not going to respond to this emergency. We have a situation where we are soon going to have robots that are capable of replacing most of you, and the robots are not going to be purchasing the stuff that they produce. That is a crisis.

Let's agree that we need to start imagining and planning for the new corporate law, for the new financial system. It is not going to emerge out of nowhere. Even capitalism was not something that emerged spontaneously. Think, for instance, about the joint-stock company. Somebody thought of it, introduced it, fought with Adam Smith (who was against it), and prevailed.

You said we don't have any ideas. Yes, we do. Imagine a market society, a liberal democratic market society without a stock exchange, where employees of Google, of Apple, of Ford, of every company, have one share and one vote. Imagine a situation where we have no private banks, because there will be no need for them if a central bank can provide you with digital bank accounts.

Allow me as a Greek very quickly to say that in ancient Athens the democrats were against elections and the aristocrats were in favour of them because they could buy them. Imagine a situation where we revisit that with more jury systems, more sortition, and more lotteries.

ARTHUR BROOKS: These are all wonderful ideas from Yanis, and it is, in fact, the truth that he's had a lot of ideas. And I'm very respectful of that, given that he is one of the most successful finance ministers in the last fifty years. He's a terrific public servant.

The problem is, how do you pay for these things, my friends? How do you pay for these things? We talk about public investments constantly. All these public investments, they're very expensive. Money is not sitting in the middle of nothing. Billionaires don't put their money in the bank or let it sit in mattresses. On the contrary, it's put to private use so that private businesses can thrive. Capitalism makes it possible for a wealthy society to fund the welfare state—to pay for these things that we're talking about.

In point of fact, you can be as politically progressive as you want. You can come up with all the ideas that you think are appropriate to lift people up. Some will work. Some won't. Some will work some places and not in others. But they have to be paid for. They don't come from magic.

What pays for every welfare program? Capitalism does. In my view, capitalism's—the democratic free-enterprise system's—greatest accomplishment is the welfare state. We're actually able to help pull people out of poverty whom we'd never seen and we'd never meet in our own society.

I know it's surprising coming from a proponent of capitalism, but that's my view. If you love your fellow men and women and you want to try new programs that will pull them up out of poverty, that will give them new opportunities, you'd better find the capital someplace. That's going to come from private businesses; that's going to come from private individuals who have the capital to pay the tax. Capitalism will get the thanks.

KATRINA VANDEN HEUVEL: As my colleague Yanis said, no one's talking about burning it down. We're trying to build it out — and build it out for millions of people who are living lives of precariousness, who aren't benefiting from the "capitalist system," the extractive capitalist system. I'm interested in what Arthur said about how we can afford to build it out, about what can be afforded in a capitalist system.

You know, the question of affordability is almost always asked when it comes to social programs that benefit those who have the least. Think about the $6.4 trillion we've spent since 2001 on endless wars that have brought us almost no security. No one asks about the corporate bloat at the Pentagon. No one asks about the tax cuts, unprecedented in a time of war, which gave money to millionaires who didn't need it. No one asks about the wasteful tax cuts we just saw and how they weren't used to invest in our country but for stock buybacks.

And I have to say, with all due respect to Arthur Brooks, that I don't think he's getting his American history right. I mean, activist government has always synched up with markets. We've needed activist government to build out the true potential of our countries. And regulations used wisely have empowered, not restricted, those who are the most valuable.

So I think we need to reassess, rethink, reimagine capitalism and move beyond what I said earlier, the cartoon characterizations. We're not talking about socialist planning. We're talking about a different kind of capitalism that will enhance its power and possibilities. Education is a good tool, but you need new infrastructure built around education and communities, housing, anti-poverty programs.

DAVID BROOKS: Everyone wants a different kind of capitalism. Irving Kristol wrote a famous book, *Two Cheers for Capitalism.* You can't give capitalism three cheers because it's based on creative destruction, and so people get hurt and you've got to have government to help give a floor to people.

What is capitalism? It's price mechanisms, it's decentralized decision-making, it's stock markets. It's investments, profit, and loss. If you don't have the stock markets, if you don't have the price signals, you can't make decisions. You're just not that smart. None of us are that smart.

And that's why socialism has failed every time. You can have widespread share ownership—I'm for that; I have shares in my company, the *New York Times,* which is doing phenomenally because of Donald Trump. He calls us "the failing *New York Times,*" and one of our journalists tweeted, "Look! We even fail at failing!"—but it turns out that most people, even if they have a share, can't make a decision collectively like a corporation can because they don't have the signals.

When you have some sort of planning, the power winds up in government, and I just am not that impressed with my political system right now. I don't trust Donald Trump enough to give him control over the economy.

Over the last few decades, the United States has seen

our economy double and our energy share the same. We're at a sixty-seven-year low of carbon emissions — it's not enough; we need to do a coal tax — but that's not because we set out to reduce energy and carbon emissions. It's just because capitalism loves efficiency and we got a good by-product out of a system that was looking after its own self-interest. This occurs again and again and again. Don't rely on the good intentions of extremely powerful people. Create a mechanism around them.

RUDYARD GRIFFFITHS: Arthur, I think one of the key issues that has emerged in this debate is your optimism about the potential for capitalism to reform itself. What I'm hearing from Yanis and Katrina is real skepticism that that is a possibility. Given the status quo they see now, many features of which you are also in opposition to, why do you think there's the potential for a positive reform?

ARTHUR BROOKS: I think the biggest difference between how I see it and how Yanis sees it is that he is more pessimistic about the possibility of capitalism becoming more democratic, particularly under current circumstances.

Why am I more optimistic? It's not because capitalism reforms itself; it doesn't. My car doesn't fix itself. Capitalism is a machine. Capitalism, socialism, any "-ism" is a structure that's not inherently moral or immoral. People are moral. We have hearts, we have brains. Morals have to come before markets, and what I'm optimistic about is our ability as a society with ingenuity to actually figure out what's going wrong and to create social movements that will make the world better.

I mean, this is exactly what Katrina and Yanis are talking about — social movements that will bring people together to get what they want. David Brooks is involved in social movements in his work. These movements are the things that actually underpin the ability of the capitalist system to be fixed. Not to fix itself, but indeed to be fixed by the imaginations, the genius, the hearts, and the minds of all 3,000 of us.

RUDYARD GRIFFITHS: Yanis, do you want to come back on that point?

YANIS VAROUFAKIS: There is no capitalism. What we have is socialism for the very, very few, and rabid conditions for an increasing proportion of the population. The "haves" are enjoying the greatest degree of socialism in the history of humanity. They have a Federal Reserve in the United States, and your central bank here in Canada, totally securing their profits during the good times and making sure that you pay for their losses during the bad times. Whenever technology produces profits, corporations use those profits in order to expand, not so much through investment in that which humanity and the planet needs, but in greater concentrated power for themselves.

We have a situation of "short-term-ism" — CEOs who are terrified of the two or three financial companies that control through pension funds the share value that determines their bonuses. So they will downsize the company immediately, independently of whether this is good for the company or not, if they think this is going to have a short-term beneficial effect on their bonuses and on the share market.

That is destroying the moral sentiments of Adam Smith. As you said, morals have to come before markets. Today, we don't have markets, we have this techno-structure with abusive concentrated power that is destroying the market. It is destroying the morality on which markets can only flourish, according to Adam Smith.

This is why we're moving in exactly the opposite way of what you are saying. And what I was very struck by was that on the side opposing the motion, on the side in favour of capitalism, you're putting forward a perfectly social democratic argument in favour of a welfare state. The problem, however, is that the concentration of power is not allowing the welfare state to survive anymore. It is becoming financially unsustainable, while at the same time the planet is becoming hotter, and our systems are failing to respond. The situation is only favouring the Trumps of the worlds, the Bolsonaros of the world, the Nationalist Internationals, the xenophobes, the racists. This is not a good environment in which democracy can grow.

This is why we need to reconsider the corporations, reconsider the financial markets. In 1944 that happened. Franklin Roosevelt convened the Bretton Woods conference in New Hampshire and redesigned capitalism into something completely different from what had existed before the Second World War. We need something similar, a reinvention to such an extent that we are no longer going to have socialism for the few and rabid misanthropy for the many.

RUDYARD GRIFFITHS: Let's bring David in here. That's a powerful, evocative argument. So, David, why are *you* optimistic about reform? Because again, Yanis is painting a picture here of powerful vested interests who really have no interest in what we might characterize as the kind of fairy-tale capitalism that you're propounding.

DAVID BROOKS: Well, first, I do think you're exaggerating the difficulties in the situation. We are in a time of pretty much full employment in this country. We are in a time of rising wages, rising wages for the bottom. As Arthur mentioned, we've pulled two billion people out of poverty. I mean, there are real signs of progress here.

Second, I've seen capitalism reform. I've seen the New Deal, which was a capitalist reform. The Bretton Woods system, the IMF, and all that—what's more capitalist?

You can go to Scandinavia if you want to make the social democratic case. I'm not sure it could work in a big diverse country like we have. But it works there. They have a high social support. They also have no wealth tax. They have no inheritance tax. They have extremely low corporate taxes. They have school choice. They don't have minimum wage laws in most of those countries. They have a very free economy.

And if you look at Denmark, are you going to tell me that's a failed state? To me, you only make big change when there's really no hope and you see no flexibility in the system. And when I see countries around the world fixing their systems, and I see think tanks like Arthur's old think tank, the American Enterprise Institute, or the Brookings Institution coming up with a zillion pretty exciting ideas—if we didn't have a moron in the White House, I could see the possibility for change. And frankly, I see a greater possibility for change on *that* side of the world than I see in a political system that is rigidifying, stultifying, and stagnating.

KATRINA VANDEN HEUVEL: I made the case that there are different kinds of capitalism, so I do think there's social democratic capitalism and I think there's Canadian-style capitalism. I think our hyper-extractive predatory capitalism is not working for millions of people. You talk about how the economy's swimming along, but millions of people are living in precarious circumstances. Home ownership is declining. Students have student debt loans to the wazoo.

We haven't talked about young people who came through the financial crisis of 2008. Among many young people there is a tendency to look at socialism, as a Gallup poll showed, as being about equality. It's not about state ownership. But people are seeking something different. And I think that, unless there is a Roosevelt—Franklin or Eleanor—New Deal 3.0, we will face a sense that capitalism in our country has *no* future.

When I think of Elizabeth Warren, to talk about our current moment, she is, in my mind, a Rooseveltian. She is trying to save capitalism as it's currently constructed from its excesses. And I think she understands that you do need to hold corporations accountable, to have a vigorous anti-corruption program, to rethink regulations. She knows where the bodies are buried when it comes to banking corruption.

The corporation needs to be rethought, as Yanis said. I began to quote the corporate leaders who understand how cancerous this shareholder primacy is to the future of the corporations. And I think that's an inflection point. Milton Friedman has ruled for too long.

So, I think about the importance of rethinking corporations, corporate power. And finally we need to think hard about the purchase of political power. The privatization of wealth and the socialization of risk come partly from the power that plutocratic elements have had in buying and rigging and writing the rules. We need to rewrite the rules and find a more democratic outcome so that we don't end up one of these illiberal countries that, David, you write about very often in your columns.

RUDYARD GRIFFITHS: I think Arthur wants to jump in on that point.

ARTHUR BROOKS: Yes. Thank you, Katrina.

There is a non-trivial irony, as Yanis points out, that David and I are talking about regulated economies. Here in Canada, even in the United States, all over the Scandinavian countries, virtually every modern economy is effectively some kind of social democracy at this point, and some programs and social democratic economies are things that people like. So, there *is* some irony in the fact that we want to preserve capitalism that can give people democratically what they want.

There's also some irony in the fact that what Yanis wants is more competition. He sounds a lot like Milton Friedman. Milton Friedman *hated* crony capitalism. Milton Friedman was *completely* against billionaires who had ill-gotten wealth. He was *completely* against the idea of privileges that come from a system that's effectively engendering landed gentry in countries like Canada and the United States that were built on principles of freedom without royalty. This is really important.

The irony is that *you* want more competition and *I'm* willing to live with more government programs. I don't think that we're that far apart—I mean, perhaps together we'll live in perfect harmony!

I think that there's a possibility that there actually are solutions to these things. The real question is whether capitalism can be saved. That's the issue that we're taking on today.

Capitalism for most Canadians and for most Americans is not large predatory corporations. It's not rich people who can get their kids into fancy universities because they went there and they have a lot of money. Capitalism is for the immigrants who come to this country and come to the United States and are able to start a business for the very first time. Capitalism is in the hearts of people who wish they were in Canada and the United States to get the kinds of opportunities that come when they can be rewarded for their ingenuity.

So, I agree with Yanis. Set the markets truly free and watch people flourish.

RUDYARD GRIFFITHS: Let's go to Yanis and then Katrina quickly.

YANIS VAROUFAKIS: I need to take you up on something you said before, which sounds completely correct. You said somebody has to pay for stuff. There is no such thing as a money tree. Correct.

But have you noticed that we live in a world where $18 trillion is in negative interest-rate territory? That means capitalism is kaput. Do you know what it means to have money that's price is negative? It's bad. People are trying to give it away and they can't. Why is this happening?

It's happening because, as I said, we have the highest level of liquidity, savings, and idle cash that is doing bugger all— excuse my French—and the lowest level of investment in the environment and in good-quality jobs around the world.

This disconnect is the signal that capitalism is broken. And this is not going to be corrected by means of more Friedman, because where I disagree entirely with Friedman is in his elevation of shareholder sovereignty above everything else. Effectively, what he was saying was that the present structure of the corporation, which concentrates more and more power until there is no room for markets to breathe, is the way in which to exercise the powers of the free market. That is where the deceit and the conceit of Friedman lies. This is why I am not a Friedmanian.

And allow me to go to somebody who is much smarter on your side of the pond than Friedman, and finish with Friedrich von Hayek, who once criticized us leftists, very cleverly saying the problem with socialists is that to impose socialism they will have to violate some basic principles of socialism.

I am saying to you that supporting the corporate structure that we have, the financial sector that we have today, is equivalent to trying to impose capitalism by means of violating basic principles of the free market.

KATRINA VANDEN HEUVEL: Let me pick up on what Yanis just said, because I could see a corporate structure where you have worker ownership and worker participation, or worker co-operatives, not necessarily corporations.

But I wanted to ask David something, because I was reading a profile of you in the Jesuit magazine *America*. My father's a great admirer of yours, so he found this profile. You said, "I'm more aware of how capitalism, unbalanced, just rationalizes selfishness . . . And it also justifies a sort of amoralism. It turns off the moral lens . . . It's made me see the ways that capitalism [has] on balance created a very shallow view of life."

So I wonder, in terms of morality — and I believe you need both moral and ethical renewal, but you also need systemic change — whether that sense of capitalism as something almost amoral has really been a part of a younger generation's view and led them to very different things than it led you to. But I wonder how you square your admiration for Dorothy Day with these comments with capitalism as constructed.

DAVID BROOKS: That's a good question. So, capitalism is morally complicated to me. I think it does arouse energy, and I think it does arouse optimism and hope. But I also think it drives a consumerist, materialist mentality. I think it also creates a hyper-individualistic privatism — "My world! Who cares about the common good?" I do think capitalist countries suffer from that.

And so, if you want to say capitalism should be your world view and your philosophy and your moral creed, I say you're going to be a selfish bastard. You'd better be a good person; you'd better have a separate creed, and a value system and a moral system that comes from a separate place, probably outside capitalism — and often pushing against capitalism. The Catholic social teaching, which I think a lot of us on this stage really admire, is that kind of creed.

In Scandinavia, there's an egalitarian creed that pushes against capitalism. And that's the way to be in the economy and be a whole person. So, when I look at communities, I look at people who are capitalists but are also deeply involved in the loving care of their community.

KATRINA VANDEN HEUVEL: So, subsidiarity and solidarity.

DAVID BROOKS: Capitalism, if regulated right, can be a very decentralizing thing.

But, let me turn around and ask you guys some

things, because there are things I'm just genuinely in question about.

I really want to know what the alternative is. I really want to understand what you're offering. First, you said that there's a lot of liquidity in the market that's not being used, and the people who control that, which in the United States are mostly pension funds, are sitting on cash because they can't find good investment opportunities.

I have three questions. My first: What makes you think you could do better and that your decisions about where that money goes are better than those of the people who now run those pension companies?

The second: I'm not really clear on where the state figures in. We've talked about worker co-operatives and co-operative buildings. How much state power are you envisioning?

And third: If every employee in the company owns shares in the company, when there's a recession does everybody suffer a loss of income? How does that larger group of people make decisions, if there's no stock market so they can't read how they're doing? How do they make decisions?

RUDYARD GRIFFITHS: Interesting questions. So, let's split those up. And Yanis, since you introduced this idea of employee ownership, how would that structure work when we have a business cycle of ups and downs, of times of recession and times of boom?

YANIS VAROUFAKIS: I'd love to answer that, but in order for my answer to make sense, it has to be part of a narrative of "How do we get there?" as well. Because the dynamics of the journey are just as important as the photograph of where you want to get to.

But I'm struck by the fact that there's no discussion about climate change here. Because, you know, we are talking about the long term. Before we get there, before we discuss the corporation of the future, we have to answer a very simple question: Where are we going to find between $8 and $10 trillion a year in order to fund the prevention of climate catastrophe?

That's where we need the new Bretton Woods. That's where we need the IMF and the World Bank to do things very differently. That requires states to collaborate. It is as hard to imagine as utopia; if you think of President Xi and Trump and the European Union, which doesn't exist—it's a figment of our imagination.

So that's part one. This is where the states have to come in, in order stabilize capitalism to make it more viable, so that we can have the transition that allows us to imagine a planet that's still there for the young generation in ten, twenty, thirty years' time.

Now to your question. First, the business cycle should not be taken for granted. These massive ups and downs of the business cycle are a product of the way in which capitalism is structured today. Especially the financial sector. The financial sector is a major booster of volatility. It borrows too much or lends too much during the good times and usually gives it to those who neither need it nor want to use it for productive purposes. And then when the bust takes place it doesn't lend to anyone.

So if we do away with the financial system that we have, that will immediately reduce the volatility. And it's a very simple idea now that we have digital technologies. You can imagine a situation where the central bank effectively gives everyone a bank account and digital tools by which to transfer money across the world, using block-chain, without needing to rely on private bankers for the payment system.

Second, imagine a situation where the state only taxes land and corporations that are socially owned. No income taxes. That's, I think, where we're moving in the future — or should move. No income taxes, no sales taxes; just taxing corporations and land.

And imagine a situation where these corporations are much, much more than they are today, because if you have one person, one share, one vote, you are not going to be having a situation where you have a Walmart that walks into a small town in the Midwest, destroys the whole eco-system of small businesses, and effectively turns everyone into a proletariat working for Walmart. That will not be possible. Then you will not have the great accumulation of profits in the coffers of Walmart that then is boosted by Wall Street, creating the boom and bust. Of course, there will always be ups and downs. But if you have a situation where we have a company of three hundred people, equal shareholders, and there are bad times, yes, we all take the hit.

You mentioned my career, my very short career, as

finance minister, and I'm very proud of that—you know what?—because I failed, and I resigned. Why? Because I was not allowing myself to sign on the dotted line of yet another extend-and-pretend bailout.

So, we need to take hits when we take them. But we must not have this turbo-charging of the volatility of capitalism, which is the result of the fact that anyone can buy shares in any company that they will have nothing to do with.

And then, of course, it's only pension funds that concentrate that ownership, and Wall Street that produces mountains of money. You know, 97 percent of money is minted by privateers. Why are we granting that power to particular individuals? This is not part of Adam Smith's mindset in favour of capitalism. We've given exorbitant power to a few financiers to destroy the planet, to destroy the world, to create crises like 2008, to continue not financing things that society needs by vesting so much concentrated power there—so the capitalism that you're defending is *this* capitalism.

RUDYARD GRIFFITHS: Let's let Arthur come in on this, because the second part of this resolution was, "Be it resolved: it's time for something different." We've just had a picture painted here of a very different reality.

ARTHUR BROOKS: Some pretty big differences to be sure. Yanis earlier reminded us of the great work of Friedrich von Hayek, the economist who taught at the University of Chicago, and who was a believer in the emergent order, that genius comes from the masses if they're truly set free.

And, by the way, when he says that he was an unsuccessful finance minister, he was a quite *not* unsuccessful finance minister. He was a courageous finance minister who stood for his principles. And that's what we need more of.

Friedrich von Hayek would listen to what we're talking about here today and say, why do you believe these schemes would work? Why on Earth do you think that these would not have unintended secondary consequences that would be massively deleterious to the lowest of the low, to the outsiders, to the marginalized, to the immigrants, to the unnamed? Why do you think that the richest people and the richest corporations wouldn't be able to game these things in ten seconds?

Because history tells us that those who are wired, those who are powerful—and this is quite correct from our interlocutors—they're the ones who resist true markets.

What we need is to set the markets free, because we need to have a bias for the people at the margins. All of the labour laws that we talk about, the minimum wage laws that we talk about, the worker protection laws that we talk about, they're very well intentioned, but remember who truly pays: the people who cannot start a business; the people who cannot live their dreams; the people who will not come to this country and actually continue to make it the freest, greatest, most prosperous society in the history of the world.

And we can't afford to take these experiments, instead of measures to set us more free and to push that freedom further out to the margins.

KATRINA VANDEN HEUVEL: I believe in freedom. But freedom is wrongly equated with the free-enterprise system as you describe it. I think those who you speak of and who we stand with — the immigrants, the most vulnerable, those who want to rise — are the ones who have gotten shafted by the concentration and the deleterious behaviour of the hyper-financialized Wall Street.

The banks are more concentrated than ever. They are not building a shared-prosperity society. I don't want to be nostalgic again about the period after the Second World War, but we know how to build a shared-prosperity society, and it had to do with government activism, state planning, higher tax rates, capital controls, and empowering workers. And that minimum wage, that didn't come just out of the sky.

So, I think we need to look back at our history, not by being nostalgic but to retrieve from our own history what is possible in order to build a different kind of system that would lift up those who you talk about, but do so in a very different way than what you describe.

I would simply add one last thing: I do agree with Yanis that we haven't talked enough about what I think is one of the existential crises of our time, which is the climate crisis. That's also about environmental injustice and those who are being hurt. And there are vast pools of unused capital that could be used to build out a green infrastructure.

And I am not one of those who just talk about climate crisis blithely. I think of the communities in this country where you need what is called the just transition. If there was more trust in government—and we need to build that—you come into a community and you build new jobs for those who fear that their livelihoods are over. Coal *is* over, but we need to make sure that those who work with coal have a future, and that their families do. But we must address the existential crisis of climate crisis.

RUDYARD GRIFFITHS: Can you come in on that point, David, on the so-called climate crisis and why you think there are market mechanisms that can address it in a meaningful, sustainable way?

DAVID BROOKS: First, we can have either a planned economy or a freer economy. The Heritage Foundation is one of these conservative free-market think tanks that rank countries according to whether they like them. And the countries high on the Heritage Foundation free-market list also have the best environmental records.

The environmental disasters that I see around the world are in China. They're in Russia. They were in the Soviet Union. They were in these planned economies run by thugs who didn't really care.

And there is something ethereal about this debate, which is that even though we're talking about the government making this transition, we live in a world of creeping authoritarianism. And so, in the actual world we inhabit, you're going to have the state led by Donald Trump or Putin or Boris Johnson making these transitions. This is the world we are dealt.

YANIS VAROUFAKIS: Why are you optimistic?

DAVID BROOKS: Well, I think we can beat them back. I think democratic capitalism is ultimately going to be better than authoritarian capitalism. But we've got to beat them back.

KATRINA VANDEN HEUVEL: David did write that he would vote for Elizabeth Warren over Donald Trump if he was confronted with the choice.

DAVID BROOKS: So, when I look at America and our environment, we have much cleaner air than we used to, and much cleaner water. We have a third more trees — it's bad for Canada, but peak logging was 1990, and our use of forestry has declined ever since. Peak fertilizer use was about 2000; we've declined our use of fertilizer ever since then. Capitalism is efficient because it pays, and innovative because it pays.

Now we need to boost capitalism along with the carbon tax. We had a very successful tactic in the fight against acid rain, which was to use cap and trade, not telling people how to fix them, because we don't really know, but making markets in pollution and giving people incentives to reduce acid rain. And it worked.

And so, to me, a global tax is the best way to unleash the creativity that none of us are smart enough to figure out on our own. I keep coming back to that core issue, and it was Hayek's point too. It's all about knowledge. It's all about how you make decisions, whether we collectively make them through a learning system, or if we sit in a room and try to figure them out. I don't have faith in that latter system.

RUDYARD GRIFFITHS: Yanis, do you want to come in on that? I think that is a key point that's come up in this debate. How can you have good decisions made by fewer people in an economy in which the millions of choices that the free-market endeavours to make every single day would be constricted by a greater role for the state in the organization and management of that society?

YANIS VAROUFAKIS: I'm not suggesting a bigger role for the state. The state has a huge role as we speak, from the military-industrial complex to the way in which, in 2008, the central banks of the world got together and created something like $8 trillion to refloat the financial system.

The problem is not that we have a small state. The problem is that we have a state that was always in the pocket of the ones who were creating the crisis, who were undermining society's sustainability and the economy sustainability.

As for the question you asked, the question you put in Friedrich von Hayek's mouth: How do we know that, if we go along the lines of reforming corporations to make it so only those who work in them own shares in them, that the rich and powerful are not going to game the system? I think the answer is in the question. Because if they can't buy shares in companies unless they work in them, then they will not be able to have corporate power.

I'm quite happy for them to have swimming pools full

of money like Scrooge McDuck in the 1950s comics—you know, they dive in and enjoy their money. I'm not in favour of taking their wealth away.

I *am* in favour of taking away their capacity to corner the markets, to corner corporate power. That is what I'm in favour of. And if you do that, then you can have a progressive shift toward more democracy in our politics, because you are going to move away from a situation where corporate power buys officials.

RUDYARD GRIFFITHS: We're going to go to Katrina, then Arthur, and then closing statements.

KATRINA VANDEN HEUVEL: David talked about people, about small numbers of people in small rooms. That's kind of the system we have at the moment, if you think of decisions being made on Wall Street.

We haven't even mentioned one of the fundamental changes in our economic system in the last forty years. I'm not an economist, but it seems that the hyper-financialization of the economy—the money making money, the fast, nanosecond speculation—led partly to the 2008 financial crisis.

As Yanis said, no one's talking about creating a huge state. There are problems that need to be dealt with at decentralized levels, at local levels, at community levels. But there *is* a place for a federal state.

I think of friends of mine who, when they learned I was coming to Canada, asked me if I'd get penicillin for them. People come up here to get drugs. And the state plays a role. And if we had a wiser state—put aside Medicare for all; that's another debate—our government would be negotiating lower drug prices. That's a simple thing. It's using its power for good.

I think the key issue we need to focus on at the moment is cleaning up our government. Whether it's Trump or a Democrat, the corruption of our government by big money, by corporate power, needs to be addressed squarely before we get too romantic—as no one at this setting is—about how good government can be. But it needs to be good, it needs to be reformed, it needs to be cleaned out, and it needs to be cleaned up.

ARTHUR BROOKS: You'll always get applause when you say the government needs to be cleaned up. And I was applauding too. Because in point of fact we have huge problems—in virtually all advanced economies and developing countries around the world—of unbelievable amounts of cronyism and corruption. We always have to find better ways to make governments more accountable, to make governments more efficient, to make governments leaner and more responsive to the people.

I don't think that making governments larger does that, generally speaking. I think that growing governments beyond what they currently are gives politicians more opportunities to get closer with the people who hold the reins of power. I think it gives them more opportunities to tax people and increase their power such that they can go according to their own interests as opposed to being truly democratically accountable to the people.

Actually, I think that spreading markets, particularly for those at the bottom, is one of the best ways that we *can* hold government to account. I'm not in favour of no government—I'm certainly no anarchist, and I'm not even a libertarian. I simply feel, and I see on the basis of what I've studied, that when I look at governments growing, they always get more bloated. When we have more policies, when there's more economic planning, there's always more opportunity for the kind of bloat that we're up on the stage tonight regretting. I don't think we can afford that.

RUDYARD GRIFFITHS: Great, thank you for that. Let's go to closing statements now. We're going to do the reverse order of the opening, so we'll put David up first. We're going to put three minutes on the clock for you.

DAVID BROOKS: So, I'm a journalist and a lot of this debate has had a bit of an ethereal feel—like we're imagining a system of blockchains and Bitcoin, of getting rid of a tax system and shifting over to something so radically different. What could go wrong?

Just off the top of my head, let's say we have a downturn. Say the business cycle has not been magically repealed and every worker takes a hit at once. Does that sound good? It doesn't sound good to me. It sounds like there are complexities that we can't even fathom.

I'm a moderate. I like gradual change. The one kind of radical change I like, and the prism through which I see capitalism, is immigration.

I was at a Latino church last Sunday with hundreds of

kids under thirty, second-generation, whose parents had come to America as so many come here, and they said, "Look how far we've come in one generation!" They were filled with joy and hope, and what they were worshipping was a lot better than capitalism. But you could see their life stories in there in the progress of a generation.

And when I saw them, I saw my own Jewish history—the butcher and the seamstress in my family—and the ocean of opportunity that hits them and is hitting people in this country. And it's caused by the growth that capitalism creates.

Capitalism has a lot of disadvantages, but people vote with their feet and migrate to free capitalist economies, to places like this city, which has been transformed since I was born here, and to my country, which has also been changed. We're becoming a multicultural mass democracy, and that's a tough shift to go through. But it's a beautiful problem to have, because people around the world in planned systems love our system. And they find a fair field and a fair chance.

KATRINA VANDEN HEUVEL: I wish I could play the Canada card. But let me try.

You know, picking up on what David said, if you wanted to realize what was once called or is called the American Dream, I say again you should come to Canada, where social mobility is at a level double that of the United States. I think that's very important.

I believe we can do better. What does that mean? We can rewire and reimagine an economy of shared prosperity that works for everyone, not just the very wealthy.

I understand that many are understandably wary of change. But I think we're at an inflection point: that capitalism as we've known it — predatory, extractive — has turned off many; it is not working for many. And that is going to lead to real change. I think we're going to see true reform or we're going to see real social discord. The centre isn't going to hold.

Since we live in the world as it is, we should also try to imagine the world as we want it to be — one in which millions live with dignity, decency, happiness, environmental well-being, opportunity, and social mobility and enjoy a new social contract, the unfinished social democratic agenda of Roosevelt, of Eleanor and Franklin, updated.

The fact is that today many fall far short of having a chance to live productive lives. And that, I believe, is deeply corrupting to the best of American values.

I do believe there is a kind of class warfare — it hasn't come up much tonight, but it's going on — and if you remember what Warren Buffett said a few years ago, in the class warfare the very rich are winning. We need just taxation at this moment. It's only fair that billionaires pay more than teachers and nurses and retail workers.

The good news is that another world and economy is possible. Many of the solutions and alternatives to extractive capitalism you've just heard tonight. So, I just want to close with words that matter to me at this moment: these are times for greatness, not for greed; a time for idealism, not ideology; and a time not just for compassionate words but for compassionate action.

ARTHUR BROOKS: There was a recently passed Roman Catholic cardinal in the city of Chicago named Francis George. Francis George once was giving a speech to his richest donors on the north shore of Chicago about funding poverty programs on the south side, and here's what he said to raise money: "The poor need you to pull them out of poverty, and you need the poor to pull you out of hell."

I'm never going to use that fundraising pitch. But ask yourself, do you need the poor? Do we need the poor? Our society does need the poor, not to stay poor but to do things that we need, and to be among us.

There are 3,000 life stories in this room. There are 3,000 family histories in this room. What do they have in common? Very little: scratching out potatoes in Ireland, running from a pogrom. In my country, many people were brought to our nation involuntarily.

But let me tell you what we all have in common in Canada and the United States. We descend from ambitious riff-raff. And we're proud of it. Why did your riff-raff ancestors come here? Because they were needed. That is the essence of dignity. That's how you become worthy of respect — to be needed. What makes you needed? I guarantee you that your grandfather was not on his way to this country saying, "I can't wait to get to where there's a better system of forced income redistribution." He said, "Finally, I'll be free. Finally, I'll be able to work and be rewarded for my work."

We need programs to help the poor. We need reform. We need to pay attention to predation. Don't get me wrong; it's absolutely true, we all know that. But fundamentally, the DNA of this system of this great country and mine is democratic free enterprise. It's the system that people still want to come to. Why do people struggle to come to Canada? Why do people struggle to get to the United States? It's because here there's opportunity.

I want more of it. I want to fix the system. I want to make it fairer. I want to make it better. But don't change the fundamental genetics of what we have that truly has blessed the world. Together we can change it, but together we need to protect capitalism as the best way to lift up ourselves and those around the world. Thank you.

YANIS VAROUFAKIS: When I was six, the secret police broke down our front door and abducted my father. I'm not a great friend of the state. But I am equally not a great friend of any privateer with excessive power over other citizens.

The one thing I learned during my political life, which started fairly recently, just in 2015, is that when a bill comes to parliament, somewhere in it you will find some vested interest that has created circumstances for the corrupt enrichment of some oligarch. If you follow the money, you will find the essence of corrupt power, of oligarchy, embedded in the DNA of what passes as really existing capitalism.

Those two experiences of mine — the first at a young age, growing up in a dictatorship; the second as a politician who has seen the way in which the financial system, the oligarchs, the corporations are destroying the lives of millions of people and are causing inefficiency and irrationality in the way we are handling our resources, both in creating opportunities for shared prosperity, especially amongst young people, and ecologically—have formed my creed.

My concerns can be summed up in one objective: democracy. The only guarantee we have, the only weapon we have against concentrated power, is a combination of civil liberties—liberty at the personal level—with democracy.

Allow me to finish off by reminding you of Aristotle's definition of democracy. It is a system of government in which the poor govern because, by definition, the poor are in the majority. What we are experiencing today is an oligarchy, a financialized oligarchy that is pushing us toward an ecological catastrophe.

We must not tear anything down. We must take every piece of technology that capitalism has created, every liberty that it has brought to us, and we should cherish it. But we need to make one evolutionary step beyond capitalism. We need to democratize economic life, democratize the way corporations are run, democratize finance—in order to save democracy, in order to save liberalism, in order to save those ideals that those who had invested in capitalism initially, two or three hundred years ago, looked upon as hope for the world. Thank you.

RUDYARD GRIFFITHS: Thank you, debaters, for a hard-fought debate. It was civil, it was substantive. We covered a lot of key issues. I've certainly been enlightened. We now have the fun of trying to figure out whose minds were changed, and what happened with this audience in terms of the arguments that you've heard over the last hour and a half.

At the beginning of the evening, we asked you where you stood on our resolution. It was 47 percent in favour, 53 percent opposed. So, a divided audience. We then asked how many of you would change your mind: fully 79 percent. So let's see the final results.

Summary: The pre-debate vote was 47 percent in favour of the motion, 53 percent opposed. The final vote showed 45 percent in favour, 55 percent opposed. Given that more voters shifted to the team against the motion, the victory goes to Arthur Brooks and David Brooks.

Post-Debate Interviews with
Moderator Rudyard Griffiths

DAVID BROOKS AND ARTHUR BROOKS IN CONVERSATION WITH RUDYARD GRIFFITHS

RUDYARD GRIFFITHS: Up first will be David Brooks and Arthur Brooks for a quick conversation to figure out how they saw this debate unfold.

DAVID BROOKS: I've been part of four debates in my adult life and this was by far the best. Substantively very rich and very strong.

RUDYARD GRIFFITHS: Well, thank you. The question I always like to have debaters try to answer is: Was there an argument on the other side that caused you to change your mind or rethink one of your core assumptions or propositions?

ARTHUR BROOKS: You know, I wish I were thinking more seriously about the predations that people are suffering from. And the argument I wish I'd made was actually made by the people on the other side, which is that we need to expose people at the very top to more competition. Because they're correct that there's a lot of socialism at the top and a lot of capitalism on the bottom. I want capitalism all the way through. It's a great point, and I'm going to think about that more, and next time I'm going to make that point.

DAVID BROOKS: I was struck by the way non-capitalism has evolved. I think that before, when you looked at the Soviet Union and so on, it was the state that ran everything and there was complete nationalization, and it was the same throughout Latin America. And so socialism was really a public-sector thing.

As for Yanis's idea, where every worker gets a share and controls the company collectively, well, I don't think that would work. I don't think they could make decisions at that level, and I don't think the companies could attract investment. There's a history where people don't invest in their futures as much in that situation, because we are human beings. And if everyone faced a recession at the same time, you would have an economic catastrophe.

But nonetheless, I do think there's a policy kernel in there to get more people invested in capitalism. And we somewhat have a national shareholder economy, including through pension plans, but not enough, so that would be a way to get people to have skin in the game. A lot of people don't feel like they have an investment in society; they think it's a rigged game. And that's a genuine problem.

YANIS VAROUFAKIS AND KATRINA VANDEN HEUVEL
IN CONVERSATION WITH RUDYARD GRIFFITHS

RUDYARD GRIFFITHS: Thank you for coming and doing this. Both of you were terrific. Part of the idea of a debate is to get people to listen to another side, because we often live in these thought bubbles, these silos of opinions. So to start with you, Yanis, which of David and Arthur's arguments would you give the most credence to? Which do you think are worthy of engagement and further thought?

YANIS VAROUFAKIS: I think this kind of adversarial positioning is a boy's game. It comes from the Oxford Union. It's quite horrid and fun, but it's a game. If we were sitting around a table, there would not be any sort of opposition, and we would be discussing the best ways to empower people and get people out of poverty.

The question—it's a semantic one, really—is what do you mean by capitalism? Would the reforms, the structure I was proposing, mean that we were really in socialism? That doesn't really matter. There were a lot of compelling arguments coming from the opposing side. I was amazed that the side defending capitalism was adopting a radical Scandinavian social democratic agenda, which I wasn't expecting in North America. This is interesting because in Scandinavia social democracies are on the wane, which reinforces the point we were trying to make that the capitalism we live in is depleting the capacity of society and of government to mind the poor, to look after the environment, and to shift power to the weak.

KATRINA VANDEN HEUVEL: And to be democratic. I was struck that neither of the Cons talked about democracy. There was little talk of what you said so well is the privatization of democracy and wealth and the socialization of risk. And I think Arthur is compelling, but his story about lifting people out of poverty is one you could challenge if you were sitting around a table. It's one he tells well. I guess I would step back and say we're at a moment, a kind of inflection point, where they know the system's not working, but they're not sure where it is going to head. So people may have thought some of what the Brooks Brothers were saying had more groundedness, whereas I think Yanis was speaking in a much more forward-looking way, looking at the root causes. And for many people, radicalism—looking at the root—is scary.

I think that often losing is winning because you lay down the groundwork, you lay down the markers, and you lay down the stakes. In terms of a debate on capitalism, being competitive is important, and we were competitive.

ACKNOWLEDGEMENTS

The Munk Debates are the product of the public-spiritedness of a remarkable group of civic-minded organizations and individuals. First and foremost, these debates would not be possible without the vision and leadership of the Aurea Foundation. Founded in 2006 by Peter and Melanie Munk, the Aurea Foundation supports Canadian individuals and institutions involved in the study and development of public policy. The debates are the foundation's signature initiative, a model for the kind of substantive public policy conversation Canadians can foster globally. Since the creation of the debates in 2008, the foundation has underwritten the entire cost of each semi-annual event. The debates have also benefited from the input and advice of members of the board of the foundation, including Mark Cameron, Andrew Coyne, Devon Cross, Allan Gotlieb, Margaret MacMillan, Anthony Munk, Robert Prichard, and Janice Stein.

For her contribution to the preliminary edit of the book, the debate organizers would like to thank Jane McWhinney.

Since their inception, the Munk Debates have sought to take the discussions that happen at each event to national and international audiences. Here the debates have benefited immeasurably from a partnership with Canada's national newspaper, the *Globe and Mail,* and the counsel of its editor-in-chief, David Walmsley.

With the publication of this superb book, House of Anansi Press is helping the debates reach new audiences in Canada and around the world. The debates' organizers would like to thank Anansi chair Scott Griffin for his enthusiasm for this book project and insights into how to translate the spoken debate into a powerful written intellectual exchange.

ABOUT THE DEBATERS

KATRINA VANDEN HEUVEL is the editorial director and publisher of the *Nation*, a leading American source of progressive politics and culture, and served as the magazine's editor from 1995 to 2019. She is a frequent TV news commentator on U.S. and international politics, writes a weekly column for the *Washington Post*, and is the author of several books, including *The Change I Believe In: Fighting for Progress in the Age of Obama*.

YANIS VAROUFAKIS is a Greek politician, economist, and academic. He served as minister of finance of Greece in 2015 as a member of the Syriza party and now sits as a member of parliament for the MeRA 25, a left-wing party he launched in 2018. He holds a Ph.D. in economics, was a Fellow at the University of Cambridge, lectured in economics at the University of Sydney, and was a professor of economic theory at the University of Athens. Varoufakis has authored several books on game theory, microeconomics, and macroeconomics, as well as the memoir *Adults in the Room: My Battle with Europe's Deep Establishment.*

ARTHUR BROOKS is a Harvard professor, bestselling author, *Washington Post* columnist, and former president of the D.C.-based American Enterprise Institute. He holds a master's degree in economics from Florida Atlantic University and a Ph.D. in public policy from the RAND Graduate School in Santa Monica. His latest book is *Love Your Enemies: How Decent People Can Save America from the Culture of Contempt*, and his other titles include the *New York Times* bestsellers *The Conservative Heart: How to Build a Fairer, Happier, and More Prosperous America* and *The Road to Freedom: How to Win the Fight for Free Enterprise.*

DAVID BROOKS is a cultural and political commentator. He is a bi-weekly columnist for the *New York Times'* op-ed page, a regular analyst on PBS *NewsHour* and NPR's *All Things Considered*, and a *New York Times* bestselling author. His most recent book, *The Second Mountain: The Quest for a Moral Life*, explores how to have a life of meaning and purpose. Brooks currently teaches at Yale University.

ABOUT THE EDITOR

RUDYARD GRIFFITHS is the chair of the Munk Debates and president of the Aurea Charitable Foundation. In 2006 he was named one of Canada's "Top 40 under 40" by the *Globe and Mail*. He is the editor of thirteen books on history, politics, and international affairs, including *Who We Are: A Citizen's Manifesto*, which was a *Globe and Mail* Best Book of 2009 and a finalist for the Shaughnessy Cohen Prize for Political Writing. He lives in Toronto with his wife and two children.

ABOUT THE MUNK DEBATES

The Munk Debates are Canada's premier public policy event. Held semi-annually, the debates provide leading thinkers with a global forum to discuss the major public policy issues facing the world and Canada. Each event takes place in Toronto in front of a live audience, and the proceedings are covered by domestic and international media. Participants in recent Munk Debates include Anne Applebaum, Louise Arbour, Stephen K. Bannon, Robert Bell, Tony Blair, John Bolton, Ian Bremmer, Stephen F. Cohen, Daniel Cohn-Bendit, Paul Collier, Howard Dean, Alain de Botton, Alan Dershowitz, Hernando de Soto, E. J. Dionne Jr., Maureen Dowd, Michael Eric Dyson, Gareth Evans, Nigel Farage, Mia Farrow, Niall Ferguson, William Frist, David Frum, Stephen Fry, Newt Gingrich, Malcolm Gladwell, Michelle Goldberg, Jennifer Granholm, David Gratzer, Glenn Greenwald, Stephen Harper, Michael Hayden, Rick Hillier, Christopher Hitchens, Richard

Holbrooke, Laura Ingraham, Josef Joffe, Robert Kagan, Garry Kasparov, Henry Kissinger, Charles Krauthammer, Paul Krugman, Arthur B. Laffer, Lord Nigel Lawson, Stephen Lewis, David Daokui Li, Bjørn Lomborg, Kishore Mahbubani, Lord Peter Mandelson, Elizabeth May, H. R. McMaster, George Monbiot, Caitlin Moran, Dambisa Moyo, Thomas Mulcair, Vali Nasr, Alexis Ohanian, Camille Paglia, George Papandreou, Jordan Peterson, Michael Pillsbury, Steven Pinker, Samantha Power, Vladimir Pozner, Robert Reich, Matt Ridley, David Rosenberg, Hanna Rosin, Simon Schama, Anne-Marie Slaughter, Bret Stephens, Mark Steyn, Kimberley Strassel, Andrew Sullivan, Lawrence Summers, Justin Trudeau, Huiyao Wang, Amos Yadlin, and Fareed Zakaria.

The Munk Debates are a project of the Aurea Foundation, a charitable organization established in 2006 by philanthropists Peter and Melanie Munk to promote public policy research and discussion. For more information, visit www.munkdebates.com.

ABOUT THE INTERVIEWS

RUDYARD GRIFFITHS'S interviews with Katrina vanden Heuvel, Yanis Varoufakis, Arthur Brooks, and David Brooks were recorded on December 4, 2019. The Aurea Foundation is gratefully acknowledged for permission to reprint excerpts from the following:

(P. 3) "Katrina vanden Heuvel in Conversation," by Rudyard Griffiths. Copyright © 2019 Aurea Foundation. Transcribed by Transcript Heroes.

(P. 11) "Yanis Varoufakis in Conversation," by Rudyard Griffiths. Copyright © 2019 Aurea Foundation. Transcribed by Transcript Heroes.

China and the West
McMaster and Pillsbury vs. Mahbubani and Wang

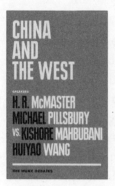

Increasingly in the West, China is being characterized as a threat to the liberal international order. For those who believe that the policies of the Chinese Communist Party pose a threat to free and open societies, the U.S. and like-minded nations must band together to preserve a rules-based international order. For others, rather than threatening the postwar order, China is its best, and maybe only, guarantor in an era of declining U.S. leadership, increased regional instability, and slowing global growth. Former assistant to the president for national security affairs H. R. McMaster and director for Chinese strategy at the D.C.-based Hudson Institute think tank Michael Pillsbury debate former president of the United Nations Security Council Kishore Mahbubani and president of the Center for China and Globalization Huiyao Wang on the threat of China to the liberal international order.

"The Chinese Communist Party's obsession with absolute control has profound implications not only for the Chinese people, but also for the rest of the world."—H. R. McMaster

houseofanansi.com/collections/munk-debates

The Rise of Populism
Bannon vs. Frum

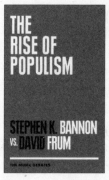

Throughout the Western world, politics is undergoing a sea change. Long-held notions of the role of government, trade and economic policy, foreign policy, and immigration are being challenged by populist thinkers and movements. Does this surging populist agenda in Western nations signal a permanent shift in our politics? Or is it a passing phenomenon that will remain at the fringes of society and political power? Will our politics continue to be shaped by the postwar consensus on trade, inclusive national identity, and globalization, or by the agenda of insurgent populist politics, parties, and leaders? The twenty-third semi-annual Munk Debate pits former Donald Trump advisor Stephen K. Bannon against columnist and public intellectual David Frum to debate the future of the liberal political order.

"I want to bring everything crashing down and destroy all of today's establishment."—Stephen K. Bannon

READ MORE FROM THE MUNK DEBATES—
CANADA'S PREMIER DEBATE SERIES

Political Correctness
Dyson and Goldberg vs. Fry and Peterson

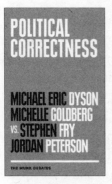

Is political correctness an enemy of free speech, open debate, and the free exchange of ideas? Or, by confronting head-on the dominant power relationships and social norms that exclude marginalized groups, are we creating a more equitable and just society? For some, political correctness is stifling the free and open debate that fuels our democracy. Others insist that creating public spaces and norms that give voice to previously marginalized groups broadens the scope of free speech. The drive toward inclusion over exclusion is essential to creating healthy, diverse societies in an era of rapid social change. Acclaimed journalist, professor, and ordained minister Michael Eric Dyson and *New York Times* columnist Michelle Goldberg are pitted against renowned actor and writer Stephen Fry and University of Toronto professor and author Jordan Peterson to debate the implications of political correctness and freedom of speech.

"Without free speech there is no true thought."—Jordan Peterson

houseofanansi.com/collections/munk-debates

READ MORE FROM THE MUNK DEBATES —
CANADA'S PREMIER DEBATE SERIES

Is American Democracy in Crisis?
Dionne and Sullivan vs. Gingrich and Strassel

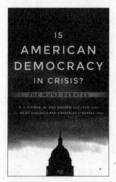

It is the public debate of the moment: Is Donald Trump precipitating a crisis of American democracy? For some the answer is an emphatic "yes." Trump's disregard for the institutions and political norms of U.S. democracy is imperilling the Republic. The sooner his presidency collapses the sooner the healing can begin and the ship of state be righted. For others Trump is not the villain in this drama. Rather, his young presidency is the conduit, not the cause, of America's deep-seated anger toward a privileged and self-dealing Washington elite. Award-winning journalist E. J. Dionne Jr. and influential author and blogger Andrew Sullivan are pitted against former Speaker of the U.S. House of Representatives Newt Gingrich and best-selling author and editor Kimberley Strassel to debate the current crisis of American democracy.

"Our country is now as close to crossing the line from democracy to autocracy as it has been in our lifetimes." — E. J. Dionne Jr.

houseofanansi.com/collections/munk-debates

Is This the End of the Liberal International Order?
Niall Ferguson vs. Fareed Zakaria

Since the end of World War II, global affairs have been shaped by the increasing free movement of people and goods, international rules setting, and a broad appreciation of the mutual benefits of a more interdependent world. Together these factors defined the liberal international order and sustained an era of rising global prosperity and declining international conflict. But now, for the first time in a generation, the pillars of liberal internationalism are being shaken to their core by the reassertion of national borders, national interests, and nationalist politics across the globe. Can liberal internationalism survive these challenges and remain the defining rules-based system of the future? Or are we witnessing the beginning of the end of the liberal international order?

"We can no longer confidently talk about a liberal international order. It's become disorder in the sense that democracy has been disrupted." —Niall Ferguson

The Global Refugee Crisis: How Should We Respond?
Arbour and Schama vs. Farage and Steyn

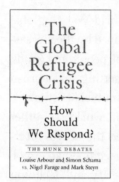

The world is facing the worst humanitarian crisis since the Second World War. Over 300,000 are dead in Syria, and one and a half million are either injured or disabled. Four and a half million people are trying to flee the country. And Syria is just one of a growing number of failed or failing states in the Middle East and North Africa. How should developed nations respond to human suffering on this mass scale? Do the prosperous societies of the West, including Canada and the United States, have a moral imperative to assist as many refugees as they reasonably and responsibly can? Or is this a time for vigilance and restraint in the face of a wave of mass migration that risks upending the tolerance and openness of the West?

"There's nothing to be ashamed of about having an emotional response to the suffering of four million Syrian refugees."
—Simon Schama

Do Humankind's Best Days Lie Ahead?
Pinker and Ridley vs. de Botton and Gladwell

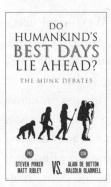

From the Enlightenment onwards, the West has had an enduring belief that through the evolution of institutions, innovations, and ideas, the human condition is improving. But is this the case? Pioneering cognitive scientist Steven Pinker and influential author Matt Ridley take on noted philosopher Alain de Botton and bestselling author Malcolm Gladwell to debate whether humankind's best days lie ahead.

"It's just a brute fact that we don't throw virgins into volcanoes any more. We don't execute people for shoplifting a cabbage. And we used to."—Steven Pinker

houseofanansi.com/collections/munk-debates

Should the West Engage Putin's Russia?
Cohen and Pozner vs. Applebaum and Kasparov

How should the West deal with Vladimir Putin? Acclaimed academic Stephen F. Cohen and veteran journalist and bestselling author Vladimir Pozner square off against internationally renowned expert on Russian history Anne Applebaum and Russian-born political dissident Garry Kasparov to debate the future of the West's relationship with Russia.

"A dictator grows into a monster when he is not confronted at an early stage...And unlike Adolf Hitler, Vladimir Putin has nuclear weapons."—Garry Kasparov

houseofanansi.com/collections/munk-debates

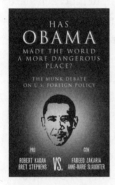

Are Men Obsolete?
Rosin and Dowd vs. Moran and Paglia

For the first time in history, will it be better to be a woman than a man in the upcoming century? Renowned author and editor Hanna Rosin and Pulitzer Prize–winning columnist Maureen Dowd challenge *New York Times*–bestselling author Caitlin Moran and trailblazing social critic Camille Paglia to debate the relative decline of the power and status of men in the workplace, the family, and society at large.

"Feminism was always wrong to pretend women could 'have it all.' It is not male society but Mother Nature who lays the heaviest burden on women." — Camille Paglia

Should We Tax the Rich More?
Krugman and Papandreou vs. Gingrich and Laffer

 Is imposing higher taxes on the wealthy the best way for countries to reinvest in their social safety nets, education, and infrastructure while protecting the middle class? Or does raising taxes on society's wealth creators lead to capital flight, falling government revenues, and less money for the poor? Nobel Prize–winning economist Paul Krugman and former prime minister of Greece George Papandreou square off against former speaker of the U.S. House of Representatives Newt Gingrich and famed economist Arthur Laffer to debate this key issue.

"The effort to finance Big Government through higher taxes is a direct assault on civil society." — Newt Gingrich

Can the World Tolerate an Iran with Nuclear Weapons?

Krauthammer and Yadlin vs. Zakaria and Nasr

Is the case for a pre-emptive strike on Iran ironclad? Or can a nuclear Iran be a stabilizing force in the Middle East? Former Israel Defense Forces head of military intelligence Amos Yadlin, Pulitzer Prize–winning political commentator Charles Krauthammer, CNN host Fareed Zakaria, and Iranian-born academic Vali Nasr debate the consequences of a nuclear-armed Iran.

"Deterring Iran is fundamentally different from deterring the Soviet Union. You could rely on the latter but not the former."
—Charles Krauthammer

North America's Lost Decade?
Krugman and Rosenberg vs. Summers and Bremmer

The future of the North American economy is more uncertain than ever. In this edition of the Munk Debates, Nobel Prize–winning economist Paul Krugman and chief economist and strategist at Gluskin Sheff + Associates David Rosenberg square off against former U.S. treasury secretary Lawrence Summers and bestselling author Ian Bremmer to tackle the resolution, "Be it resolved: North America faces a Japan-style era of high unemployment and slow growth."

"It's now impossible to deny the obvious, which is that we are not now, and have never been, on the road to recovery."—Paul Krugman

Hitchens vs. Blair
Christopher Hitchens vs. Tony Blair

Intellectual juggernaut and staunch atheist Christopher Hitchens goes head-to-head with former British prime minister Tony Blair, one of the Western world's most openly devout political leaders, on the age-old question: Is religion a force for good in the world? Few world leaders have had a greater hand in shaping current events than Blair; few writers have been more outspoken and polarizing than Hitchens.

Sharp, provocative, and thoroughly engrossing, *Hitchens vs. Blair* is a rigorous and electrifying intellectual sparring match on the contentious questions that continue to dog the topic of religion in our globalized world.

"If religious instruction were not allowed until the child had attained the age of reason, we would be living in a very different world." — Christopher Hitchens

READ MORE FROM THE MUNK DEBATES—
CANADA'S PREMIER DEBATE SERIES

The Munk Debates: Volume One
Edited by Rudyard Griffiths
Introduction by Peter Munk

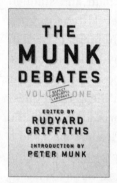

Launched in 2008 by philanthropists Peter and Melanie Munk, the Munk Debates is Canada's premier international debate series, a highly anticipated cultural event that brings together the world's brightest minds.

This volume includes the first five debates in the series and features twenty leading thinkers and doers arguing for or against provocative resolutions that address pressing public policy concerns such as the future of global security, the implications of humanitarian intervention, the effectiveness of foreign aid, the threat of climate change, and the state of health care in Canada and the United States.

"By trying to highlight the most important issues at crucial moments in the global conversation, these debates not only profile the ideas and solutions of some of our brightest thinkers and doers, but crystallize public passion and knowledge, helping to tackle some global challenges confronting humankind."
—Peter Munk

houseofanansi.com/collections/munk-debates